How to be a Brilliant Primary School Head Teacher

A simple, practical guide to leading a primary school for the very first time

Gary Nott

Brilliant
PUBLICATIONS

Publisher's information

Published by Brilliant Publications Limited
Unit 10, Sparrow Hall Farm
Edlesborough, Dunstable
Bedfordshire, LU6 2ES, UK

Website: www.brilliantpublications.co.uk
Tel: 01525 222292

The name Brilliant Publications and the
logo are registered trademarks.

Written by Gary Nott
Illustrated by Frank Endersby

Printed ISBN: 978-1-78317-300-6
epdf ISBN: 978-1-78317-301-3

First printed and published in the UK in
2018.

Contents

Section 6: Teaching and Learning

Section 7: Communication

Section 8: Finance

Section 9: Health and Safety and Safeguarding

Section 10: When Things Go Wrong

Section 11: What Next?

Section 12: Head Teacher's Calendar

Introduction

I always wanted to be a head teacher. I was fortunate enough to be appointed a deputy in my twenties and to my first headship in my early thirties. Now twenty years, four schools and ten inspections later, those nice people at Brilliant Publications have invited me to reflect upon the highs and lows of my career, pulling together thoughts for this book in the hope that they may prove useful to aspiring Heads, newly appointed Heads or even tired Heads. In addition to my own schools, I have been executive head at two schools that were in an OFSTED category. I learned a great deal from these experiences. Working in a school that is in a category is tough, very tough and the people who do so have my utmost respect. Whatever type of school you lead – community, voluntary aided, faith, free or academy – I hope there is something of interest for you in this book, which has been written in a conversational style and is divided into sections so you can dip in and out or read from cover to cover.

Before You Read This Book, Know Four Things ...

Firstly, I like telling stories. I tell a number of stories in this book, some of which you might like to use in assemblies with your pupils. That would make me smile. They are – I should add – tried and tested with primary aged children; OFSTED even sat in on them. The inspectors said they liked them, which is always a good sign!

Secondly – headship is a highly personalised game. I make no grand claims about this book. It is a collection of personal views assembled through my own particular experiences. Experienced colleagues will no doubt disagree with many of the viewpoints contained within. This book is not for them; they will know it all already and much more besides. I wrote it because when my deputy was promoted to headship, I wanted to buy him a simple practical little guide about leading a primary school for the very first time. Try as I might, I could not find one entitled, 'My First Headship' – so here is my humble attempt to fill a perceived gap in the market.

Thirdly, growing up I wanted to join the circus. Yes, really. I never made it. Being a head teacher has perhaps been the next best thing! There are some circus analogies in the book, which are signposted with this motif.

Finally, most primary schools are rated 'good' by OFSTED. This book tries to show you some of the ways you might set about taking such schools to outstanding status.

> I have put these in **BOLD** in borders like this.

Are You Ready for Headship in a Primary School?

> 'Talent alone won't make you a success. Neither will being in the right place at the right time, unless you are ready. The most important question is – "Are you ready?"'
>
> Johnny Carson

When is anyone ready?

A simple answer might be, 'When others say I am!' – or, perhaps not. When I was first appointed a deputy my then head teacher said in a reference that I 'wasn't ready'. I only know this because somebody later told me. In retrospect, I think he was probably right in that I wasn't ready to do the job; however, I was perhaps ready to start learning to do it and to some extent you can only do that when you are in those shoes – meeting those opportunities and making those mistakes – and hopefully achieving small successes that sustain you.

You won't necessarily know if you are ready.

The real question is do you want to have a go?

If you feel ready for that, then there is nothing holding you back.

'You're on!'

Section 1: Your First Headship

You are – to some extent – on your own now!

Prologue: What now?

'A good beginning makes a good ending.'   English proverb

So you've got the job. Congratulations!

You'll feel like celebrating. And, so you should. It is no mean achievement. But at some point, the enormity of what lies ahead will hit you. You're then bound to question if deputy headship has prepared you well for what is to come. That will depend upon how much you have been involved with the day-to-day running of your former school and how much you have influenced the big decisions. Some head teachers involve their deputies in one, but not the other. Others include them in both. In the light of your own experience, now might be a good time to ponder on how you will treat your future deputy. But, let's put that to one side for a while and address it in a later chapter.

Your new school will be keen for you to visit before you take up your post. Some newly appointed head teachers elect to get fully involved before they officially start; others prefer to stay at arm's length until they take up the reins– they fear that being on site when the incumbent Head is still around will inevitably cramp their own style. Personally, I liked to know the essentials that I needed in order to hit the ground running in September, but no more than that! I didn't feel the need to meet either the children or staff informally or otherwise. I wanted to keep my powder dry. I wanted the first impressions I was to make to be on my own terms.

However, I did want a profile of my staff – their perceived strengths and weaknesses (this would enable me to decide which year groups they would occupy in the new school year – very much a decision that I wanted to make). In addition, I wanted:

- an overview of the budget – where there was money that I could look to spend differently to fund early projects of my own (where I could therefore make a mark);
- details of any vacancies that I would have to fill;
- the strengths and weaknesses of particular cohorts and where the priorities for development therefore lay;
- the most recent RAISE data – again showing me where areas for development lay;
- an analysis of the last action plan – where milestones were reached and where areas remained outstanding;
- the most recent post OFSTED action plan;
- the last newsletter (to see what the parents are used to)

All that, remember, before I was in post. Nobody said it was going to be easy. Far from it: fun, but not easy.

Your Non-negotiables (well almost!)

In journeying to this point you will have formulated a philosophy of what you believe in, what education should be for and how it should be delivered. There are plenty of academics who write much about the subject. When I think back to my first headship, I had ten principles that I held dear:

- education was about the whole child;
- excellent behaviour and attitudes to learning were the cornerstone of everything;
- fun should be at the heart of the curriculum;
- there should always be a place for discovery learning;
- consistency was key – be 'persistently persistent' as my first Head told me;
- setting by ability in reading and maths was important;
- children should be encouraged to work in teams;
- talk for learning was crucial – if you can't say it you can't write it;
- policies are there to be followed – better not to have one than not to follow it;
- the primary history programme of study should not be dominated by facts; despite what some politicians argue, enquiry skills are just as important.

You will want to have some non-negotiables. You have earned that right in getting to where you are. One colleague whom I coach said that they learned quickly to stick to their guns. I would say that is fine, but be prepared to bend and change. Time and experience will help you to do that. It isn't a weakness to move away from a position you would have once defended to the hilt. Circumstances, or as one colleague eruditely put it, 'the educational landscape' will change and you will need to change with it. A week was famously described as a long time in politics – the adage holds true for education.

I still believe in all of the above. But after twenty years there are other things that I am aware of. Other masters who must be served.

If I were rewriting my non-negotiables, a further two would feature and they would perhaps come top of the pile:

- test results are paramount, but it matters how you get there;
- financial stability is key – it allows you to accelerate change.

Your First Day

You will need to decide what it is you want to get out of your first day at work. Don't aim too high.

A head teacher colleague that I coach told me that they didn't know on the first day where the A4 paper was kept before a colleague wanted to talk to them about their contract.

Go at your own pace. And at this early point, it is good to get yourself acquainted with three handy phrases:

'Leave that with me, so I can give it some proper thought. I'll get back to you tomorrow.'

This will buy you time. You can't expect to have all the answers as soon as people need them. After all, it may have taken them a while to think of the question; you should be entitled to the same time to find a response. Say something off the cuff and you may regret it. And if you do shoot from the hip and immediately think better of it – when the person has stepped out of your office – track them down and say, 'I've thought better of that, leave it with me... (well you get the idea). But – and this is a warning – do make sure you get back to them when you have said you will. If you don't, they won't forget it.

Secondly, never underestimate the usefulness of the phrase:

'What about you, what do you think?'

Often the person who has the question will already have an answer and it may be better than anything you can think of. Job done! You don't have to be the font of all knowledge. Even if they don't have an answer, it buys you some thinking time and the fact that they don't have an answer shows it may not be an easy problem to solve.

Thirdly, discover the most useful word in a head teacher's vocabulary.

"Interesting"

Question:	Why don't we stagger lunchtimes?	Answer:	Hmmn, that's interesting.
Question:	Why don't we teach maths to boys and girls separately?	Answer:	Hmmn, that's interesting.

It's non-committal, but equally, not dismissive.

You may need it on your first day, when some staff will want to put to you their burning idea for change – one that was usually rejected by or not even voiced to your predecessor.

Elsewhere on the first day, you will want to stand up and be counted – to make an impression. Your first day together will likely be an INSET day. You will need a set piece – something to introduce yourself to your new team. This should be the whole staff, not just the teachers. The latter would give out the wrong signal. You are a team and you are all in this together.

It needs to be short. And you need to be gentle. Now is not the time to frighten anyone.

I suggest twenty minutes, tops. Spend the first ten, telling them where they are going. Spend the second ten, telling them the sort of boss you will be and how, therefore, you will help them get there – together. To do this, you could usefully use the story of the two circus owners that appears later in this book (see page 24).

Then, an idea would be to hand over to other core leaders to deliver key messages in their subject areas – what is going well with a hint of where improvements could follow in coming weeks and months. You need to signify to staff that this is not a one person effort – rather, that it is all about the team!

Then give the remainder of the time over to teachers to help them prepare. There will be a lot for them to do and they will appreciate the gesture. Headship is all about gestures. Show staff that you remember what it was like to be a busy teacher.

As you drive home on your first day, remember a golden lesson that will stand you in good stead. Thrive on the positives from the situation. Yes, there will be things that didn't go as you had hoped, but if you dwell on them, you will be losing before you have started. There are always positives, albeit small ones on occasions. Focus upon them for they will motivate you and add to your confidence. A confident head teacher – not an arrogant one – is something all staff want!

'I think that went rather well...'

How to be a Brilliant Primary School Head Teacher

Your First Fortnight: Get to know your team

> 'Sometimes it takes a while to find that perfect balance between knowing who you are, what the right sound is and building the right team to make that happen.'
>
> **Judith Hill** (American songwriter)

Make it a target to meet with each member of staff during your first fortnight in charge. This is their opportunity to tell you what they liked and disliked about the previous way of doing things. If you take more than a fortnight it will appear to delay the new start that you have been planning and some of them may have been hoping for. Here are some questions that I have found useful in such discussions:

- what do you want me to know about you?
- what did you like about working for the previous Head?
- what three things would you change about the school, moving forward?
- what sort of Head do you want me to be?
- where do you see yourself in three years' time?
- if I overheard colleagues talking about this school under the previous Head, what would they be saying?
- if I was talking to the previous Head about you, what would they say? What would they report your strengths and weaknesses to be?
- are you proud to be a member of this school?
- do you think the school needs a new direction, or do you want more of the same? – some will!

The answers to these questions will tell you a lot. They will reveal whether there is appetite for change and in what areas. They will also reveal where there has been frustration – always good to know. You should include all staff – teaching and non-teaching in order to get a round view. If you don't take this opportunity to formally invite comment, some staff will be keen to let you know informally what they think whereas others will be less forthcoming – this will skew your impressions of the school you are inheriting. Far better to hear what everyone has to say.

Your Introductions

Firstly, to the parents

This can be done in four ways during your first week in the job.

Firstly, get out to the gate and shake some hands. Ask parents how they are and ask which year their child is in, and their name. Don't get drawn into long conversations. It will stop you talking to others and may put you in a difficult position: a parent might be looking for something in particular from you that you may or may not wish to promise; offer them an appointment in such circumstances. If you are not comfortable with small talk – some people aren't – just smile and wave.

Secondly, you can write to all parents to introduce yourself. This is an important opportunity and requires some serious thought. The letter, which should be one side of A4 no more, should give the parents a taste of you and of the things to come. It should go out on your very first day in charge – people will be expecting it.

It should include:

- a passing reference to the previous Head, thanking him/her for all they have done to lead the school to this point (never criticise them);

- say how pleased you are to be joining the school;

- talk a little about you and your family – you want parents to see you as a rounded individual who experiences the same challenges in life as they do;

- identify three commitments: changes that you personally intend to bring about by July – go for crowd-pleasers; if you can, choose one thing that the previous Head had denied them but you feel comfortable with introducing (you'll have to do your homework to find out what this might be) – but be subtle though.

Thirdly, introduce morning surgeries: a slot, say 8.30–8.45 each day, when you are available to meet with parents without an appointment. This goes some way towards the open-door policy that parents so like. But it also makes the point that you can't turn up at 2.00 o'clock without an appointment – unless, of course, it is a genuine emergency.

Fourthly, in my first week, I also introduced an email account called tellgary@sky.com. This meant parents could always gain access to me day or night. And some did! Eventually, I had to shut the account down because I attracted some unsavoury anonymous posts. It was a shame, because many parents liked it and took positive advantage of it. I have recently reintroduced it with a less provocative gary.nott@redbridge.gov.uk.

Secondly, to children

If you're going into a school where behaviour is already great, you can look to build upon that, without being heavy handed. If there is work to be done, at some stage you will need to set out what your expectations are and stick to them – then be 'persistently persistent'. But try to resist the temptation to shout or even raise your voice (interpreted by many children as shouting!) There's really no need: parents and children don't like it. So stay calm and be firm but fair.

Your first assembly is key. First impressions count. I can remember sitting in an assembly where the new Head started off his tenure by listing his 'rules'. It didn't play well. The children immediately saw him as grim and a disciplinarian and it was a tag he struggled to shake off. It begs the question, how do you want the children to perceive you? I would suggest you want them to see you as someone who commands respect but can be great fun. So maybe in your first assembly, you could tell them a little about you (and your family) and then say what you have liked so far about the school (in this way you are setting your expectations but in a positive, praising manner). Your second assembly, at the end of the same week should make them laugh (a little – don't go over the top!)

This is a great one to send them off to the first weekend liking you, which is very important for a head teacher.

Miss Galvin's Story (an assembly story for children)

Miss Galvin was a popular teacher. She had arrived at St. Peter's direct from Australia. The children had warmed to her instantly and the staff quickly embraced her into the life of the school. She spoke with a funny twang that endeared her to the children. There was a lot to learn: English schools being different to Australian ones. But she put a huge effort into learning new ways.

The autumn term came and went with all the usual events – harvest festival and Christmas. When she came back to school in the New Year, she wondered how she might make her mark on the school. She knew the remainder of the year would fly by and at the end of the summer she should be returning to Australia. She wanted to find a way of ensuring the children and staff at the school would remember her.

As she sat in the staff meeting on the last day of spring half-term, Kerry Donaldson – English lead teacher – was talking about how the school would celebrate the forthcoming World Book Day. They were to have a Roald Dahl theme that year. All the children would be encouraged to dress as a Dahl character, the staff too. This would be her chance: she would dress in a costume that was so memorable the children would remember her long after she had gone. Later, sitting in the living room, she was surrounded by Roald Dahl stories and characters: the Twits, the eponymous Charlie, George and Matilda. And then she hit upon it. She would dress up as Agatha Trunchbull from Matilda. What a character! She was said to look 'more like an eccentric and rather bloodthirsty follower of the stag-hounds than the headmistress of a nice school for children.' She read the passages of the book carefully that described her appearance. She was said to be muscular and mean.

That Saturday, she shopped for her outfit. She found a tweed suit and once home she put it on. She looked great. She would add make up on the big day, which was Friday week. She was excited at the thought.

'Who are you coming as, Miss?' Simon Jenkins had asked her.

'It's to be a surprise, Simon,' she replied. 'Just think "The Child Catcher" from Chitty Chitty Bang Bang and then add a heap of trouble with a cherry on top.' She chuckled at the thought.

That Friday morning of World Book Day, she rose early and dressed as her character. She expertly applied make up and set off for work in her car. She took a change of clothes with her in a holdall; the costume was hot and she would be glad to change out of it at the end of the day. She felt more than a little self-conscious. At the traffic lights, she drew up against a mother with her three children, who couldn't stop starring and pointing at her. They clearly didn't know whether to laugh or be frightened – they stared on incredulously.

She was glad to escape their gawping faces and shortly pulled into the school car park. She took her phone from the dashboard. There was nowhere to put it – the costume had no pockets and so she carried it in her palm and, popping into the staffroom, placed it safely in her pigeon hole.

The day was great fun.

All the children in her class came dressed and they were mightily impressed by her costume, which they judged 'cool!'

As she waved them off at the end of the day, several parents came to her and thanked her for making such an effort. She smiled inwardly. The day had been a success.

She made her way back into her classroom and glanced at the clock. It was 3.30. It was time to get out of the costume and change into something cooler.

She picked up her holdall and went into her walk in cupboard, which stood at the back of the class. She closed the door behind her and locked it. Wearily, she took off each item of clothing, putting them into a neat pile. Then she slipped on the summer dress and comfy shoes. Although it was stuffy in the cupboard surrounded by piles of books – and truth be told, there wasn't much room to manoeuvre – she already felt cooler. She reached for the door handle and gently pulled.

Nothing.

The door stayed where it was.

She pulled harder.

Still nothing.

And then harder with both feet on the door and both hands on the handle.

A bead of sweat erupted on her forehead and she panicked. The door wasn't going to budge, she could tell.

A cold fear set in on the hot afternoon.

She banged on the door and hollered.

'Can anyone hear me? I'm trapped.'

She reached for her phone. She would call for help. How clever was that!

Then she remembered she didn't have her phone. She could see it in her mind's eye sitting in her pigeon hole.

She yelped.

'Can anyone hear me?' she wailed. 'I am locked in my cupboard.'

She banged again.

Nothing.

She put her back to the door and slid to the floor, crumpled. Was she to be left here all weekend until Monday morning when the school would return? There was nobody at home to raise the alarm for she lived alone. She thought hard. She had arranged to meet up with a friend on Saturday afternoon. They would be worried when she didn't show. They may even visit her home and find no one there. They would be bound to be concerned. Might they even contact the police? Victoria groaned at the thought. How embarrassing. A man hunt might ensue. Or in her case, a silly teacher from Australia hunt!

She sat on the floor for what seemed an age but when she looked at her watch, only an hour had elapsed. It had seemed like a lifetime.

She banged again. She wailed. She cried.

Elsewhere, sitting in his classroom marking books, Mr Jenkins thought he could hear a muffled banging coming from somewhere. He must be mistaken. There was nobody about, most staff having left promptly after school, it being a Friday. It had not been his day. For some time he had been meaning to conjure up the courage to ask Miss Galvin out on a date. He had been sweet on her since setting eyes upon her in September. She didn't seem to notice him. She was friendly towards him, yes but there was nothing to suggest she shared his attraction... . He followed the sounds, muffled and not consistent. What could it be? A water pipe he thought maybe blocked with pressure building up. He had known radiators and pipes to make all sorts of noises.

He stopped in the corridor. There it was again, a thundering this time. Was it coming from class 3G? From Victoria's class?

He entered the classroom and listened.

Silence.

On the other side of the cupboard door Victoria had all but given up. Nobody was going to hear her. She was trapped and would remain so till Monday when her class would return. Would she even be alive then, she thought. She laughed to herself; now she was being silly. People survived for much longer when lost in the desert.

In the classroom, Andrew Jenkins pinched himself. He thought he had heard someone laugh.

Had it come from the cupboard at the back of the room?

Cautiously he approached.

He stood at the door. All at once, he felt silly. He was imagining things.

There was nothing for it.

He knocked and timidly asked, 'Is anyone there?'

From the other side of the door came a yell and a hurried sound of movement.

'Yes,' cried Victoria, 'I am.'

Andrew pulled the door and it opened without a struggle.

Victoria emerged, relieved beyond what words could say.

There seemed only one sensible thing to do: she kissed Mr Jenkins there and then. A great smacker of a kiss right on the lips. He was all at once her prince and on that Friday evening, he had rescued her. For one of the two colleagues, it had been their lucky day!

Section 2: You as a Head Teacher

'A bit retro I know, but I think a powerful
statement nevertheless... '

Know What Motivates You

> 'Life is 10% what happens to you and 90% how you react to it.'
> **Charles R Swindoll**

It is important to identify what motivates you. Maybe, you could usefully reflect on what got you to this point. So we stop momentarily for the first of some brief activities. At this point it might be helpful if I explain that I follow the talk-do-talk-do approach that characterises the outstanding lessons I have been gratified to observe – more of that later. If you just read, your attention will waver. If, by contrast, I punctuate the book with a number of activities, we stand a chance of you remaining engaged. You will need to do roughly the same amount of reading to complete the book but you will stand a better chance of assimilating what I am attempting to say: some activities then, each one lasting no more than a few minutes.

1 | **Activity One:**
Take a few minutes to identify what motivates you – what have been the drivers in your search for a headship in a primary school? Are they the same ones that inspired you first to be a teacher? List them before you read on.

- So what do we have?
- Did you mention money?
- Are any obvious ones missing?

If we were in the business sector, I think we could have expected pay to feature more prominently. But it doesn't in most head teachers' lists. Can you think why? The answer is simple: head teachers aren't paid significantly more than deputy head teachers in most primary schools – enough for a new car or holiday, but not both.

But I think motivation is a good starting point because knowing what motivates you will allow you to have an insight in to what you say and do. Know thyself, as the proverb says.

2 | **Activity Two:**
Find three people you trust. Ask them what they think motivates you.
Was there any commonality between their responses?
Were there any disappointments for you?

How might you approach the future differently? Perception is key! It doesn't matter if you think colleagues were wrong in their assessment of you. At the end of the day, that is how you are perceived. If you don't like it, resolve to do something about it!

Motivation matters: it will determine the actions you take. It will be transparent for all to see.

A New You!

> 'Ultimately leadership is not about glorious crowning acts. It's about keeping your team focused on a goal and motivated to do their best to achieve it, especially when the stakes are high and the consequences really matter. It is about laying the ground work for others' successes, and then standing back and letting them shine.'
>
> **Chris Hadfield** (Astronaut)

As a deputy you will have developed a certain style, whilst enjoying certain successes and making some mistakes too along the way.

Headship is a fresh start. You don't have to be the old you. You can be something different.

So now is a good time to take stock and decide upon the leadership style you want to adopt in your new role.

There are plenty to choose from, and whilst it is true that we all instinctively bring a certain amount of baggage to any role, this is still a new beginning. Provided that is, you are starting in a new school. However, that said, even if you have been promoted from the deputy role within your own school, people should not expect the old you – they won't necessarily, though some will be tempted. This is headship: it's different to a deputy's role: the buck, I'm afraid, stops with you and as a consequence, everything changes. You will come to see the world differently and in time people will see you differently too.

What styles of leadership are open to you?

Hay McBer, through research, identified a set of leadership styles. There are plenty of other models out there. If you Google leadership styles, you will be overwhelmed. I like the Hay McBer template because it can easily be applied to schools.

Hay McBer characterised the leadership behaviours that they witnessed as falling into six styles:

Style	Typically...	Advantages and disadvantages
Coercive	I'm in charge	Useful for schools in crisis and fire drills but even then many counsel against it
Democratic	Let's decide together	Takes a lot of time to come to decisions and the tough decisions (ie unpopular) decisions might not get made

Authoritative	I'm in charge but I'm listening	Probably the most common style in primary school where most heads are comfortable – consultation, yes, democracy, no
Affiliate	I want you to do it because we like each other	Tricky. Bonhomie only gets you so far. Some authority, it can be argued, is necessary
Coaching	I'm going to show you how it can be done	Takes time and patience but reaps rewards
Pace Setting	I'm going to keep us moving forward together	Dynamic – relentless

But the one, I would argue you want as the leader of an outstanding primary school is missing. The one that is most characteristic of outstanding schools and is often referred to as 'servant leadership'. The term was coined by Robert K Greenleaf in his essay 'The Servant as a Leader' but it is an age old concept.

What is it and just importantly, what is it not?

It is not, as one leadership applicant once described it to me, a bottoms up approach. (I think he meant bottom, singular – the use of the plural provoking a rather amusing if not a little disconcerting image.) The style pulls upon some of the characteristics from a few of the Hay McBer models. The key, for me is in the motivation. Sometimes they will be leading from the front, at others times, bringing up the rear. But, what motivates a 'servant leader'? It is not self-importance, or power or position. However, you can perhaps claim the title if your greatest satisfaction comes from the success of others and their achievements. You might be authoritative, democratic or even at times a little coercive. But your motivation is key and it will explain your actions and attitudes. Since my own school was judged by OFSTED to be 'outstanding', my governors have been quick to congratulate me. To which I invariably reply, 'It's a team effort'. That's not false humility. It is a team effort and nothing gave me more pleasure in the report than to see my leaders and managers celebrated. Their success is what motivates me. Servant leadership is about taking pleasure in enabling others to 'shine', putting yourself second.

You should decide upon the leadership style that will pervade your school. You won't be doing it alone – but you will take the lead.

Linked to this notion of servant leadership is Goleman's emotional intelligence. How is this strand of intelligence described?

It's all about being in tune with one's emotions and those of others. Knowing one's strengths and weaknesses and 'importantly' one's drivers is vital;

understanding why you do the things you do. Being able to change course in order to respond to changing events is key, picking up on the undertones when working with colleagues. Being good with people is essential, being able to move them in the wanted direction and, importantly, putting oneself into other's shoes when coming to decisions.

Just how important is it for you as a school leader to have emotional intelligence?

Here is a tale of two circuses. Both are doing rather badly and both welcome new ringmasters one season. In the first circus, the ringmaster leaves no performer unshaken. He sets new ways of doing things. His expectations are high. There are stern rebukes for those found wanting. And very quickly, it becomes a case of shape up or shift out. The aerialists lose their nerve; the clowns lose their sense of humour; and the animals become restless and nervous. The crowds pick up on the performers' discomfort and sit uneasily in their seats. Bit by bit, the crowds grow smaller and the circus folds. The ringmaster blames the acts that he inherited; they simply weren't up to the grade, he says.

Meanwhile, in the neighbouring town, the second ringmaster has a different approach. He too has high expectations but makes it his business to get to know his performers. Gradually, he instils in them new belief. He shows them how they can make the tricks sharper and their animals keener. He convinces them that there is no better life than that of the circus; and the crowds, picking up on the performers' obvious contentment and good spirits, grow.

The second ringmaster I would suggest was emotionally intelligent. The first was not.

It is said that Emotional Intelligence is four times more potent than IQ

Outstanding primary schools have 'inspirational head teachers and other leaders'.

What makes them inspirational? The answer? Simply put, people say they inspire them. The apple is in the eye of the beholder. And what will make people say that about you? Nothing more so than the degree to which you empathise with them whilst getting the job done. In short, your level of emotional intelligence will be high.

Are you emotionally intelligent? If you don't know, how might you find out?

And if you're not. Can you become so?

Yes.

Never Let Anyone Pigeon Hole You!

When I was first a deputy, the Head decided all staff were to have some feedback on their styles. We were each asked to use five words to describe one another. We were encouraged to be honest. There were a lot of people sweating, I can tell you. I was described, the Head told me, as intelligent, articulate ... yes, as you can imagine I was enjoying it... but then he followed with 'demanding', 'arrogant' and 'sometimes a bully'. The 'bully' one hurt. But looking back on me then I can see I was brash and immature – I was after all only 27. My father, who had gone to work at 14 and become a father at 17, and was working every hour sent, would say my age was no excuse!

Later, when I was first appointed to headship my styles were analysed by 360° feedback. My propensity to coach (work alongside me) was quite high - 65th percentile. My affiliation (do it because you like me) was low at 25th percentile. My democratic (let me involve you as an equal partner) tendencies were rock bottom at the 12th percentile. My coercion (do it because I say so) was through the roof at the 99th percentile. I ran my school as though it was in special measures. It wasn't.

One of the staff commented that they thought 'I was in it for myself'. That hurt. I wasn't, essentially. But it was fair, looking back, to suggest that I was going to drag my staff screaming and kicking to where I wanted them to be: I wasn't in it for myself, I was in it for the children. In putting them first, my default position was that the staff had to come a firm second. And I guess if I am being honest, I was in it for me, a bit – headship was an unconscious ego trip. I was not a servant leader and I was most definitely emotionally unintelligent!

Recently, I found myself in therapy and was invited to ask five work colleagues to choose three words to describe me: placid, compassionate and resourceful, were each used by more than one colleague. What had changed? Well, I had. What had changed me? Life! I had come to realise that it wasn't enough to deliver the goods; I had to take people with me if I was going to feel any sense of satisfaction. My first head teacher used to say that if people disliked you, was it because you were either doing your job or not doing it? If it was the former, he argued, you could sleep at night.

Today, I take the view that if you can't deliver for the children and keep the staff happy and liking you, all at the same time, then you are in the wrong job. Nobody gets in the car wanting to come to a school that is not happy. Happiness matters: big time!

I make this point only so that you know whatever sort of a leadership style you have employed up to now, it can be altered. If, that is, it is not where you want it to be. You decide.

> **Your school won't go from good to outstanding, without servant leadership infusing all levels of the organisation.**

Dealing with the stress

At the same time, you will need to take care of yourself. I have been a head teacher for twenty years, a deputy for six and during that time I have had two break downs: times when I had become so stressed by the job that I couldn't cope and carry on. It happens to the best of us. I have seen colleagues fall by the wayside, where they didn't just bend, they broke. You need two things to complement your work. Firstly, you need a mentor and then you need a coach.

A mentor will generally be someone who can help you make quick fixes, model to you how to do things – usually for a head it's a more senior colleague. However, a coach, if you can get one, is usually someone not only outside the school but outside education. Someone who does more listening than talking. Someone who will see you in the round – be able to talk to you about how you are feeling, how you are coping with the pressures that come your way. In the absence of a coach, it is usually a spouse who comes closest to fulfilling this role.

Consider the following prompt sheet that might be used to guide a discussion between a coach and their colleague (page 27).

Record of coaching for a leader

Tell me about an issue you are facing at the moment – a challenging problem, a difficult colleague...	
How are you thinking about solving the issue?	
How are you feeling about the issue?	
Are there alternative routes?	
Is your confidence high?	
How might you make it higher?	
Do you have any negative thoughts regarding the problem?	
How might you resolve these?	
Is there anything else you want to discuss today?	
What do you want to achieve by the next time we meet?	
Are you clearer about how you are going to get there?	

Long Term

What drives you? What is your long term motivation?

Recent research by the Centre for High Performance and published in the Harvard Business Review, looked at actions taken by a sample of academy head teachers. They were looking at what it takes to turn a school around. Your first headship may be to a school in such circumstances. If it is, you will be on a fast learning curve.

They found that head's actions in such circumstances could be categorised and people fell into one of five types of head teacher:

- **Surgeons**: take immediate steps to boost exam performance by excluding poor performing students and instead concentrating efforts on those pupils taking exams. Are typically PE or RS teachers
- **Soldiers:** focus upon improving school finances in order to develop the school. Keen to minimalise costs by cutting support staff and non-essential items. Are typically ICT or chemistry teachers.
- **Accountants:** look to expand the school to strengthen it. Seek new ways to generate income. Are typically maths teachers.
- **Philosophers:** contemplate values and sharing ideas around teaching and learning but typically do not achieve notable developments. Are usually English or language teachers.
- **Architects:** not interested in quick fixes. Take a long-term view and make sure the climate is right for improvements. Centre upon pupil behaviour, augmenting income and improving teaching and learning; usually delivers better exam performance. Generally studied history or economics.

The study concluded that Surgeons' impact is rapid but not maintained; whereas Architects deliver long-term improvement.

So what will you be?

It's all about motivation – what drives you. Are you in this for the long term and why? If it is to see others become successful and to gain a sense of satisfaction from that, then headship is the job for you. If it's all about you – power and influence and money – then the headship of any school might not be for you after all.

Don't forget, by being a head teacher in a primary school, there will be opportunities to *serve* people. A **servant architect** will be a challenging route to take but ultimately a rewarding one in terms of job satisfaction.

Take a few minutes to read the following story. It shows that teachers who come to school bring baggage with them. You, as a servant leader, will need to be ready to help them lift and carry that weight. Are you up to it? Read the following story to see why you might need to be emotionally intelligent in your role.

Annie's Tale (a story for grown-ups)

The morning had started early. They had started to do that regularly of late. She looked across at the alarm clock, which blinked 3.31 am. She rubbed her eyes. Surely it couldn't be that time. Scott was awake in his room; she could hear him – he had turned on his television. He was watching Toy Story 3; she could hear Buzz and Woody's voices floating down the stairs and that of Lotso bear too. She said a little prayer. Please don't let it wake the baby. She waited, holding her breath. Then she heard Maddie cry. She sighed. Sleeping next to her, snoring and oblivious to it all, lay her husband. She quietly slipped out of bed and tiptoed up the stairs; one child was still asleep, at least she hoped so. 'Shhh,' she whispered to Scott, passing his door, 'turn the television down or you'll wake Tom.' She went to Maddie's room where she found her eighteen month old daughter who was looking at her over the edge of her cot, crying. Sweeping her daughter up into her arms, she cuddled her to make the tears stop. They didn't, so she quickly descended the stairs and juggling the baby in one arm, she took a bottle down and filled it with milk from the fridge with the other hand. She then slipped back into bed and pulled Maddie tight. Upstairs she could still hear Scott, who was whooping now. She thought back to when her husband and she had first noticed that Scott was different. He was two and a half, and wasn't talking. The diagnosis of autism, which came a year later, had winded them, like a blow to the stomach. Now seven, Scott attended a special school in the next town. She realised that he had turned the television back up, this time louder. She glanced over at the clock. 4.30. Tom might wake. She lay there, watching the numbers flick over on the clock. Maddie was now asleep again but she herself couldn't rest. She was worried about her husband. He had been working too hard lately. He had first been diagnosed with OCD as a teenager. He lived with it on a day-to-day basis; he had learnt that he just had to get on with it – there was no choice. But from time-to-time, it would flare up, the rituals – the checking – and he would need her. He needed her now. She knew that when he awoke, he would be looking for reassurance from her with what was worrying him that particular day. She had made an appointment for him to see his doctor. She would go with him that evening.

He was drinking too much; he said the alcohol relaxed him but she worried – worried because he was on medication for the condition. Her mother had agreed to look after the children that evening for an hour or so. She would hurry home from work to get him to the doctor's by 5.00. It would be a push but doctors' appointments were hard to get and she could bring her marking home with her. He looked so peaceful as he lay there, free from the worries that would later cloud his day.

'Mum,' came a voice. It was Tom. The noise from Scott's room had woken him. Slipping Maddie off her chest, she rested the toddler carefully between her husband and a pillow, positioned to stop her rolling out of bed should she stir. She made her way up to Tom's room, again pausing outside Scott's, who immediately turned down the volume when she asked him to: he was a good boy, he just found life more difficult than most. She made her way down the corridor to Tom, who was sitting up in bed, looking troubled. 'Scott woke me,' he said. Then he burst into tears. 'Why Darling, whatever is it?' she asked, searching his face for some explanation. 'I'm worried about the spelling test today. Mrs Cuthbert shouts so if your score is poor. She frightens me.' 'Mrs Cuthbert,' she voiced with a sigh. She knew the teacher only wanted the best for her students but there were different ways of doing things. She would hate to think that any of her own pupils were scared of her, their teacher. 'We'll get up in a little while and practise them over breakfast,' she said, pulling him close. 'Now try to get a little more sleep, it's early' – she turned the light back off and pulled the door quietly shut.

Back down stairs, she removed the pillow that had substituted for her now cold body, and slipped back into bed. Maddie stirred but did not wake. From upstairs, she could discern that Scott had turned the volume back up on his television. She glanced across at the clock – 5.30. It would soon be 6 and time to get the chores done. She tried to doze off but couldn't. Her sleep had been disturbed and that was it, damage done. A short while later, packed lunches made, she called Tom. 'Time to get up darling,' she said. Her voice floated up the stairs. No response. Likely as not, he would have fallen back into a deep sleep and would be grumpy when she had to wake him. Why did Scott have to get them up so early?

Her husband stirred. How was he? 'I think it might be going to be one of my bad days,' he said sheepishly. She kissed him on the forehead. 'Never mind,' she said, we have Dr Davies this evening. 'He's always so helpful. Go and shower and we'll talk it through over breakfast.'

Tom, she called for a second time.

'Coming,' came a bad tempered response. Eight going on thirteen, she thought. Kevin and Perry.

Scott ate his toast in front of the computer and Maddie nibbled on some flakes strapped into her chair in front of the television. Tom and George, her husband, sat at the breakfast table, both looking glum. In between testing Tom on his spellings, she sought to reassure her husband. Yes, it was true he was under a lot of pressure at work at the moment. The doctor would see that she felt sure.

'Scott, time to get your shoes on darling, we'll be going in a moment. Tom, shoes and teeth.' Maddie, she realised, needed to be changed. Her husband called out his goodbyes as he shut the door. 'Do you have your lunch?' her words chased him out of the door. He hadn't. She rushed out to press it into his palm.

With Maddie strapped in, they clambered into the car, the three of them.

7.30. She turned the key in the ignition.

A whirling sound but no contact. The car had been playing up of late but she had not managed to find the time to phone the garage. She said a little prayer and tried again. Contact – the engine sprung into life. She turned out of the drive and headed for the car park of the King George pub, where Scott's bus and escort would be waiting to take him to school. It was an arrangement they had come to only recently. Tom's school was nearby and it made sense to do the handover there rather than wait anxiously for Scott's bus to get to them at the house on time. Scott safely despatched, she drove Tom to St Mary's. There was always a ten minute wait before the school gates opened. She tested Tom on his spellings whilst they were sitting there. He looked worried and her heart went out to him.

8.00. The breakfast club doors opened and she kissed Tom goodbye.

It was a short drive to Auntie Ann's; she could do it in less than ten minutes if there wasn't any traffic. There was. It took her fifteen minutes. She glanced anxiously at the clock. 8.20. Auntie Ann was waiting for her on her drive; she deposited Maddie into her waiting arms and then dashed back to the car. If she put her foot down she could make it to school by 8.35. The pupils would start coming in at 8.50. There would be just time to set the class up for the day. She walked into Reception glancing up at the clock. 8.30 – she realised that she had been up for over five hours.

Mr Jenkins, the Head was waiting for her in reception.

'You have remembered that I am observing you first thing this morning, haven't you Annie?' he said.

She hadn't.

She burst into tears. Sitting in his office later, she felt just a little silly and ashamed.

What was he going to say to her?

What would you have said?

And what would that have said about you?

Behind each member of staff is a life. A life that will invariably feature all sorts of pressures. Whether it be caring for a young family or an elderly relative – or both! You must be prepared to see beyond the professional. A head teacher colleague once said to me, 'I expect them to leave their personal baggage at the door'. I couldn't disagree more. Get to know your staff and support them with their private lives. As head teacher you will need to be mentor, coach, confidante and above all, human. You will get far more out of staff, if they know you see the whole person.

'Mother, do you think the Head sees the real me?'

The Power of Positive Thinking

In my experience, the difference between successful and less successful colleagues is not that the more successful ones have fewer setbacks, it is how they approach those setbacks. The better colleagues see them as an opportunity to grow and get stronger. For others it becomes a case of doom and gloom. The first head that I worked for used to talk to me about the power of positive thinking. I think what she meant was we create our own luck – using setbacks as stepping stones to something better. It's an art. You have to work at it. But, it's infectious: if you do it, your team will catch-on.

Of course, when we talk about luck, some colleagues at first sight appear luckier than others – in that they work in seemingly more favourable settings. I used to think there were two types of headship, both involving feet. There was the 'put your feet up headship' and conversely the 'work your socks off headship'. You know the kind of thing. In the former, the children came in brilliant and left brilliant – sometimes despite, not because of, the teaching they received. Then there was the other kind of school, where the children came in well below average and left significantly above because of the outstanding teaching they received. I say I used to think that because I have recently become a governor at what I would have perceived to be a 'put your feet up kind of school'. How wrong I was. How can such schools begin to show that they add significant value when the starting points are far higher? It can be done. We know that because there are schools that do it. But it is just as hard as showing value added to lower starting points. You might argue harder.

All headships bring challenges, whatever the context. There are no easy schools and consequently no inherently lucky headships. Make your own luck through positive thinking.

**Leafy suburbs can have it tough too.
Add value to that!**

Section 3:
The Role of the Head Teacher

'No one told me it would be this glamorous...'

The Head Teacher is a Team Member

'Two heads are better than one.'   English proverb

As a leader, at any level in a primary school, we will find ourselves a member of a team. So it makes sense to have some appreciation of team dynamics – what makes them tick.

In his work Belbin identifies nine roles needed for a team to be firing on all cylinders. As I describe them now, can you identify with one or more of them?

- The co-ordinator, who oversees the workings of the team. They will be experienced and secure in themselves. Might delegate rather too much;
- The implementer, who can realise the goals of the team;
- The shaper, who motivates others – demands a great deal and may not suffer fools;
- The plant, who is creative but not necessarily good with people;
- The resource investigator, who can track down items that the team needs;
- The monitor/evaluator, who will drill down and be efficient but who may be a glass half-empty person;
- The completer/ finisher, who will get the job done;
- The team worker – good with people, does the work on the ground – puts the hours in;
- The specialist, who brings important skills but who may not buy into the team's goals.

Belbin's work is inevitably a list of stereotypes that may not always apply to the people with whom we have all worked in the primary school, but it has some uses as a discussion point in our sector.

Now, let's consider you. You are, essentially, the point of this book.

3

Activity Three
Try to identify yourself within Belbin's group of stereotypes. Where do you fit? List yourself in rank order on a sliding scale of 1–9: 1 being the role that best describes you (in your opinion), and 9 being the role that sums you up least well.

4

Activity Four
Now let's try to decide which characteristics are the most important to have as a head teacher in a primary school. Rank the nine roles again, where 1 is the most important within the context of leadership and management of the head's role in school, 9 the least important.

Was the task easy?

I guess you struggled. I know I did.

But why, in any case, am I getting you to distinguish your own strengths as an individual in terms of the different roles, when Belbin tells us that a 'group' of people, not one individual, will be needed to represent all nine roles in an effective team? Well, you will need to be able to make the strongest contribution in your leadership team because you, as head teacher, will need to be able to make up for the team's shortfalls in terms of Belbin's list. It's a good idea to know your strengths so you can work on your weaknesses – you will need to be an all-rounder – nothing less will do.

In addition, to be an effective head teacher in a primary school, you will need bits of all nine because at times you may be needed to steer a particular project from conception to completion – alone. Others, who may already be stretched in other directions, will want their say but they will expect you to be in the driving seat – making the pace, setting the momentum and completing the task.

This leads us nicely on to an examination of the differences between leaders and managers. For again, you will need to be both.

Leadership and Management

5

Activity Five

Write down three most important characteristics of effective leaders; then the three of effective managers. By 'characteristics', I mean what they are, not a description of the activities that they do. Consider what you have written. Was it easy to distinguish between the two?

If you had to pick out just one key quality of a leader and then a manager, what would they be? Decide before you read on.

For me, if I had to pick one for leadership, it would be that leaders have original ideas. Leaders initiate change. I am reminded of that great little poem by Roger McGough:

I wanna be the leader
I wanna be the leader
Can I be the leader?
Can I? I can?
Promise? Promise?
Yippee I'm the leader
I'm the leader

OK what shall we do?

And in terms of management, the trait I most admire is the ability to manage people – not money – not resources – business managers can do that – if you encourage, and let them – no, the real challenge is to set the right conditions that will allow people to shine! For managers sustain the change that leaders initiate; and people are at the centre of their hopes and aspirations.

Hay McBer describes the attributes of an effective leader as:

- analytical thinking
- challenge and support
- developing potential
- drive for improvement
- holding people accountable

- impact and influence
- information seeking
- initiative
- personal convictions
- respect for others
- strategic thinking
- team working
- transformational leadership
- understanding the environment
- understanding others

6

Activity Six
Pick your strongest three attributes?
Would others say the same about you?
Does what you think matter when compared to their thoughts?
Perception, after all, is the key. If they don't perceive you to be these things, will they be ready to follow you?
Without followers, you won't be much of a leader.

Now let's think about Leadership as opposed to Management.

Does being good at one imply being good at the other?

History tells us that some leading figures were effective leaders, while others were effective managers – being good at one does not necessarily imply being good at the other. The two facets are not mutually inclusive.

James I
Great leader: good ideas man; wrote about the evils of smoking some three hundred years ago!

Poor manager. If a bridge needed building in Leeds, he wanted to be involved. I exaggerate to make the point. Hopeless at delegation.

Winston Churchill
Great leader but lost the post-war 1945 election because the electorate judged that he didn't have the ideas to lead post-war development. Mismanaged the election.

Henry VIII
Great leader. Broke with Rome: innovative!
Poor Manager: Needed Thomas Cromwell to
manage the changes for him.

Charles I
Great Leader: Bold, ideas man.
Poor Manager: Lost control of parliament. Lost his head!

Moses
Great leader. Could capture and motivate minds: lost control of his people, who
began to worship false idols in his absence – mismanagement on a large scale.
Consequence: those people would never see the Promised Land.

7

Activity Seven
Can you think of someone in your school experience who led well but
managed poorly. Or vice-versa?

What made them the person they were? Or weren't?

Now think of someone who not only led well but managed well too.
Are you thinking of yourself, by any chance? You'll get a chance to
prove it in the coming months.

I digress with a little more circus!

 When I was first appointed to headship, I saw
the leadership role as akin to a 'trick cyclist' –
a unicyclist. You may know the type.

The wheel represented management within the school.
The sorts of things the Head managed: school staff;
curriculum; budgets; resources; relationships with
children; pupil behaviour; involvement of governors;
accommodation; community relations; liaison with
feeder schools; training; technology. It's quite a list.

You will no doubt spot things I have missed.

All that managing was going on and crucially it was the Head who was doing it and at the same time had his or her feet on the peddles – charting the course and the pace of change – in other words leading too!

I have moved away from that model over the years.

First to another type of circus cycle act. You know the one. When a dozen or so people clamber on to one bicycle and go round the ring together. This model did at least acknowledge that it was a team effort. There were more of us managing – problem solving, budgeting, evaluating, monitoring, dealing with conflict, negotiating, planning, organising, interviewing, writing, delegating, decision making – but it was still the Head who was leading – had their feet on the peddles – dictating speed – and I was of course in control of the steering. Not much had changed in effect.

Finally, – maybe I should say eventually – I have come to see leadership as a head teacher differently. I have left the cycles behind and now see my role as more akin to that of a ringmaster. I welcome the public into the tent and then provide some continuity between acts: where each performer shines as they never cease to amaze and amuse. And as with all the best circuses, there is huge audience participation, both in the ring and from the vantage point of a seat in the audience. What you control as the ringmaster is the pace of the show and in the same way the speed of change in a school. This is vital, for the pace of change will determine ultimately how successful it is. Nobody emerges from the show, talking about how good the ringmaster was. The acts decide together which direction the performance will take. The ringmaster is there to lend a guiding hand. As it is with circuses, so it should be with schools. The less noticeable the Head is, and the more remarkable the pupils and staff are, the better the circus – sorry, the school, we run.

Managing Your Own Time

Another significant challenge will be to manage your time. If you can't manage yours, how do you expect to manage that of others? They will look to you for a pervading sense of calm. Deliver that and you will inspire confidence – another key to your success.

I like to think of Time Management being as simple as A, B, C and D.

A stands for action. 'Just do it,' as Nike says. It may be important to you and therefore the arguments for 'just doing it' will argue for themselves. It may however, seem unimportant to you but if someone has asked you do to it, it will no doubt mean something to them. If it can be done quickly, even if it appears trivial, just clear it off your desk by doing it.

B stands for Bin it. It might be interesting. But not interesting enough. And if all it's going to do is go into an endlessly rising pile, you might as well dump it now rather than later. It will leave you feeling lighter.

C stands for consider. This one is for stuff that is interesting and you can envisage yourself doing something with it at some point – but not just yet. Be judicious though – is it really one for the bin?

D stands for delegate. If you are going to be effective as a head teacher in a primary school, you will need to delegate. Think James I and that bridge (see page 38). If you try to do everything, you will fail. There is simply too much to do. And secondly, how will others feel if you are not seen to trust them with important stuff?

Your desk: Keep it tidy. I know the old adage 'Empty desk, empty mind' but visitors to your room (especially secretaries) will interpret an untidy desk as belonging to someone who is disorganised. This may or may not be true but you wouldn't want them to think it.

Diary: I don't keep a diary. No, really, I don't. The school secretary keeps a school diary, which serves to note all my movements as well as those of other leaders and 'school events'. In this way, we all know what we are each doing. I meet with my secretary to run through the diary at the start of each day.

Meetings: In time, you will begin to discern which meetings you need to attend, which it would be impolite not to attend and those which you should avoid. Head teacher colleagues won't like it if you don't attend the meetings that they attend: it will suggest that you think they are wasting their time – sometimes, they are. Many of your own staff won't want you to be out of school at meetings. 'Any excuse,' some will say, 'to get out of the building.' It is true that some head teachers spend far too much time on what I call 'foreign policy'. It serves no purpose, however, to become closeted in your own bubble even if you are confident of what you should be working upon.

Workload

> **'The Head never got it. I was working all the hours God sent, and not always on the right stuff.'**   **Experienced teacher**

Hmmm, this is an interesting one!

A good head teacher cuts back on every level of bureaucracy to leave time for planning, teaching and marking. That is what teachers should be doing – and they should be doing it thoroughly. Here are some examples of what they should not be doing:

- photocopying;
- entering data into spreadsheets;
- displays;
- gaps analysis from test papers;
- making labels;
- completing risk assessments
- filing;
- collecting money;
- sorting medication;
- tidying;
- chasing absence letters;
- sharpening pencils (yes, I've seen them doing it).

Other people can do these things.

And meetings ...

Staff only need INSET periodically, certainly not very week – even for staff who are under-performing; if you have people who need additional training, make it during the school day. You can overdo it in terms of after school INSET! Be bold, be different. Yes have a short briefing each week but a main INSET only every other week – and none in June, when teachers have reports to write. If you can halve the number of full meetings staff attend – it remains doggedly at one a week in most schools – you will be well on your way to helping them achieve the coveted work/life balance.

What About The Head's Workload?

I have tried to identify some of the many things that you should be doing as a Head but where, do you ask, does your work/life balance come in? Of course, it is important you have one. Even if you put many of the strategies into place that are outlined in this book, there will be times when you become all consumed. It's that sort of job. But if you are to have any longevity, you will need to take steps to keep a balance. At the time of writing, retirement age stands at 67. If you are appointed by the age of 40, that's some considerable time to survive! With all the best intentions, events can overtake you and you can lose sight of the fact that you should have a life outside your job. This is important for three reasons. If the job is all there is in your life, the demands you make of others will become unreasonable. Secondly, children and staff want an interesting person as their Head. You won't be that person if the job is the sum total of your interests. Finally you will need a support network that for most of us is a loving family. I have a colleague whose children sometimes tease her that she spends more time with the children in her class than she does with them.

There will be times when you have to put your family first.

And just occasionally, yourself!

Jack's Tale (a story for grown-ups)

Jack knew he had forgotten something. It was bothering him. He had been so busy at work lately that he seemed hard pressed to look up and see what was going on around him. It was niggling him, this thing he had forgotten. He was up before the family and in the car before any of them had stirred. It was an hour's drive to work and he liked to be in before other colleagues.

Today was going to be difficult. The relationship between his deputy and senior leaders had broken down. They were hardly speaking. It was placing a strain on the whole team, who were all too conscious of the disagreement. He resolved to speak to his deputy before school – see if he couldn't pour some oil on troubled water. The problems had stemmed from a recent residential. Although he had heard of friends going on holiday together and falling out of friendship whilst away, he hadn't heard of colleagues being similarly affected. But they were where they were.

'Look Tom,' he ventured. 'Sometimes we have to apologise even when we haven't done anything wrong.'

'Can't do it,' replied his deputy.

'Look, Jemima thinks you are bullying her.'

'Bullying, I'm not even talking to her. How can I be bullying?'

'I think that's her point,' Jack replied. 'Not talking to someone is a form of bullying in the workplace.'

He could see his deputy was genuinely surprised by this interpretation.

'I'll apologise,' he said. 'Just as long as you acknowledge that I have done nothing wrong – nothing intentionally at any rate.'

Jack sighed with relief. It was a weight off his mind. He returned to his list of things to do. The pen in his hand hovered over the paper. He knew he could have added something but couldn't for the life of him remember what it was. It was still niggling him.

There was a knock at the door. It was Tracey Williams.

'Jack,' she began, 'I think we have a problem.'

'Natalie Dower has alleged that Mum and Dad hit her with a stick when she is naughty.'

Jack sighed. This day wasn't getting any easier.

'Are there any marks?' he enquired.

'A very faint line, I couldn't tell you if it had been made by a stick.'

'Let's have a chat with her.'

Moments later, Tracey was ushering a seemingly confident Year 2 child into his office. Wide eyed she sat back confidently in the chair and gazed around, drinking in the surroundings like a teenager draining a milkshake from a glass with a straw.

'Have you been in my office before Natalie?' he ventured.

'No Sir,' she answered, beaming.

How to start? He was always apprehensive in such circumstances. He knew the drill. No leading questions. An open discussion that went where it wanted. Always tricky.

'Tell me about what you like at home.'

'I like to play with my toys.'

And is there anything you don't like at home?'

She seemed to know where he was going with it. After all, she hadn't been to his office before. He guessed it wasn't a huge leap for her to make: she had said something to Mrs Williams that might have been shared. She repeated her disclosure. She didn't like it when Mummy hit her with a stick.

He stopped. He wouldn't probe further. That would be for Social Care to do.

Natalie bounced out of the office with her teacher and he made the referral.

At lunchtime, he grabbed a bite from a sandwich but quickly pushed it under some papers when there was a knock at his door.

It was Gill.

'Can I have a word,' she said – shutting the door.

She burst into tears.

Gill was one of three secretaries but the only one with children at the school.

'It's about this letter,' she said, her voice trembling with emotion. 'It says that Stephanie is not making adequate progress in her reading. I'm doing all I can but the letter makes me feel like a bad parent.'

He took the letter from her and invited her to sit.

'I don't know why I am crying. I feel stupid but once you start, you can't stop!'

He scanned the letter. He could see her point. It was generic – a one size fits all kind of thing – designed to get parents reading with their children. But Gill did that; he knew it, she knew it.

He apologised.

Not for the first time that term.

She looked happier as a result of his comments.

The silence was interrupted by a piercing wailing. The fire alarm. It would be one his more errant Y6 boys, flexing their muscles with just three weeks of the school year left.

Both he and Gill rose and made their way to their different duties.

Once back inside, he found himself opposite Tommy O'Sullivan. He had bragged to classmates that he had been responsible. A one day fixed exclusion was the inevitable outcome. Tommy didn't seem bothered, nor would his father be, Jack thought. Part of the problem.

The phone buzzed. It was Social Care wanting to talk about Natalie. Tommy was ushered out of the room by his deputy. Social Care would be visiting just as soon as they had spoken to the police. Did they realise that school finished in just under half an hour? The duty worker explained that he would have to keep Natalie at school and away from her parents until they had had a chance to speak with her. That would mean a difficult phone conversation with Mr or Mrs Dower.

On balance, Mr Dower was quite reasonable. He appeared to realise that Jack had a job to do and that the processes had to be followed. He said he would speak to his wife and said they would wait for a call later that afternoon.

The police officer who accompanied the social worker seemed calm and methodical.

They spoke to Natalie and she repeated the story. She would be hit with a stick that was kept in the garden.

'When had the last time been?' she was asked.

She couldn't remember.

'Had a hit ever left a mark?'

She couldn't remember.

'Was she frightened to go home that evening?'

'No.'

Tracey took Natalie out to wait in Reception.

The police officer phoned her father. He put it to him that Natalie had said she would be hit with a stick.

Jack listening to the police officer's conversation could tell that Mr Dower was strongly denying the accusation.

He put the receiver back down.

'Something doesn't seem quite right,' he said.

'Let's talk to Natalie again, this time without staff here.'

Jack and Tracey waited in Reception.

A short while later the policeman emerged with Natalie, who was still smiling.

'Can we have a quick word, Sir?' said the officer to Jack.

Back in the office, the officer relayed that Natalie was now happy to say that she had made up the allegation. She did, she had said, make things up from time to time. She didn't know why she did it. The officer was proposing to accompany Natalie home when her parents arrived to collect her. He wanted to check there was no stick where Natalie had purported there to be one but his gut was telling him that this was a false alarm.

What a day!

Jack sat at his desk. It was now a quarter to seven.

He called home.

His wife answered.

She was disappointed in him, he could tell. He had been late home before; it was one of those things. He would leave now.

At just after eight, he walked through the front door.

He was met by shrieks from his two young children and his wife emerged from the kitchen door with a cake in her hands, candles lit. 'Happy Birthday, Darling!' she said.

And there it was. What had been niggling him all day. He had forgotten his own birthday.

His wife tousled his hair.

'It could have been worse,' she laughed. 'You might have forgotten mine!'

This job, he thought, it takes over your life.

'Daddy,' said Abbie, his young daughter. 'Next year, will you promise to come home early on your birthday? We missed you!'

He made the promise.

As he fell asleep that night, he said a little prayer that he would be able to keep it. You just never knew.

Accountability

Is there a profession in England that is more scrutinised than that of the classroom teacher? Teachers' performance is annually evaluated formally by their senior leadership team. There are lesson observations, work and planning scrutinies, learning walks and pupil progress review meetings. Other professions' performance is held to account in their own way. Fair comment! However, teachers are also scrutinised by OFSTED at least every three years – unless their schools are deemed 'outstanding'; even then, such schools live with the spectre of a poor risk assessment triggering an inspection after three years of securing the accolade. Their pupils' assessments may be published online and reprinted in the local papers. Each term, a local authority inspector will come calling – cue for more observations and learning walks. (If you are a member of a Multi Academy Trust, such a function will be picked up by the Chief Executive or someone working for them.) And for final good measure, a teacher's performance is discussed each evening and morning at the school gate (or even online) by the parents – the 'consumers' – in a way that customers don't gather daily outside the local supermarket or bank to discuss the employees who dwell within. Doctors aren't scrutinised in the same way, nor the police.

It is your job as head teacher to protect your staff from the worst of these excesses. You can make a start by not referring to OFSTED every two minutes, tempting though it may be. And if the Local Authority assigned inspector makes a visit, they must be contained. Too many of them like to act as pseudo-OFSTED inspectors. Your observations of colleagues teaching should be limited to once a term – the same goes for planning and work scrutinies. Progress reviews should be supportive – an exploration of what you can do to support them in their efforts; such meetings must not resemble something akin to the Spanish Inquisition.

A Hierarchy of Attributes for Modern Headship

What would you place here?

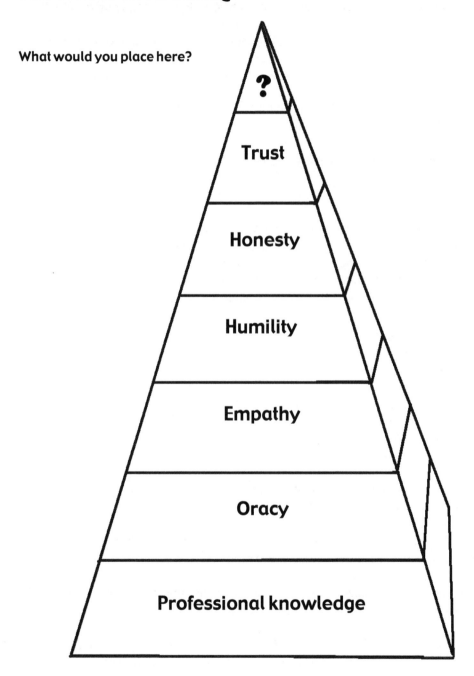

?

Trust

Honesty

Humility

Empathy

Oracy

Professional knowledge

Leadership in a Faith School

> **'I was never sure about leading a faith school although I had a faith. It seemed too daunting.'**
>
> **Catholic colleague working in a non-denominational school**
>
> (There are literally hundreds of such colleagues.)

Some colleagues will be leading in a faith school and this will bring an additional dimension to their work.

Let's start with one small piece of scripture:

As you read it, try to identify why I am choosing to begin with it:

Then Jesus made the disciples get into the boats and go on ahead to the other side of the lake, while he sent the people away. After sending the people away, he went up to a hill by himself to pray. When evening came, Jesus was there alone; and by this time the boat was far out in the lake, tossed about by the waves, because the wind was blowing against it.

Between three and six o'clock in the morning Jesus came to the disciples, walking on the water. When they saw him walking on the water, they were terrified. 'It's a ghost!' they said, and screamed with fear. Jesus spoke to them at once. 'Courage,' he said. 'It is me. Don't be afraid.' Then Peter spoke up. 'Lord, if it is really you, order me to come out on the water to you.' Come,' answered Jesus. So Peter got out of the boat and started walking on the water to Jesus. But when he noticed the strong wind, he was afraid and started to sink down in the water. 'Save me Lord,' he cried.

At once Jesus reached out and grabbed hold of him and said, 'How little faith you have. Why did you doubt?'

 As a head teacher in a faith school you will notice strong winds, but it is my firm conviction that the Lord will be there to grab you.

 There will undoubtedly be times as a head in a faith primary school when you will be called to walk on water. Peter did it, so can you!

This books talks about some of the facets of leading a primary school. There are some obvious links to be made with Christ and how He lived his life.

The first would be servant leadership, as discussed earlier in the book.

Jesus said that he came to serve, not be served. The washing of the Apostles' feet is a representation of this. It doesn't mean, of course, that Jesus would not lead at times through example – that he would forever be bringing up the rear. Jesus did lead from the front – quite literally, on more than one occasion when he had to go back to get the Apostles because they were at first hesitant to follow. But he did so for the right reasons: to embolden others, to give them the strength to lead the right life.

Secondly, we are given an excellent example in the Gospel of the importance of effectiveness as opposed to efficiency – explored further in a later chapter.

Let's consider Martha and Mary's encounter with Jesus to make the point.

> As Jesus and his disciples went on their way, he came to a village where a woman named Martha welcomed him into her home. She had a sister named Mary, who sat down at the feet of Jesus and listened to his teaching. Martha was upset over all the work she had to do, so she came and said, 'Lord, don't you care that my sister has left me to do all the work by myself? Tell her to come and help me!'
>
> The Lord answered her,' Martha, Martha! You are worried and troubled over so many things, but just one is needed. Mary has chosen the right thing and it will not be taken away from her.'

Martha was busy being efficient; Mary was preoccupied being effective.

The Gospel holds many parallels for our lives as leaders in faith schools. I have been a head teacher in both faith and non-faith schools and there is a difference, believe me, or at least, there will be if you are going about it the right way. In a faith school, everything one does is done in order to mirror the Lord: to show others that there is a way of leading and managing that sets us apart. That is not meant to sound smug and self-important but it is an important assertion. It's not meant either to suggest that people in maintained schools aren't kind to one another, or look out for one another. But getting the job done in a faith school isn't enough and being kind to one another as one goes isn't sufficient: in a faith school, in leading and managing, we must try to speak to others of our faith – what it means to be a follower of Jesus.

Section 4: School Improvement

How to be a Brilliant Primary School Head Teacher

Your First Month

An outstanding school is clear about where it is going and how it intends to get there.

You will need both a vision and a mission statement. Everyone has them: from your doctor's surgery to your local post office. A vision statement should be a pithy one liner: your goal – what you are trying to achieve. The mission statement is in some ways trickier. It is a statement of how you intend to deliver your stated vision – a way of working. It could usefully be a paragraph. The formulation of one is a great way for everyone to buy in to what you are trying to achieve and can begin to cement a team. There are dangers though. You could give people a blank sheet, which may intimidate or in some cases 'spur on'. I say spur on because your team may come up with things to which you don't subscribe. What then? You either disappoint them or go against your better judgement. Whose school is this? Well it is theirs as much as yours, in a sense. You are in this together. There is after all, no point leading if no one is following you.

How else could you move forward in its formulation?

You could give a draft. This will inhibit some – the cynical will see it as a *fait accompli*. And then it begs the question: why are you doing this unless you want to hear what people really have to say?

You are probably best advised to spend a whole day on the exercise. It could be one of the most productive days you will spend together, if well managed.

Establish the vision first. What is your school aiming for?

I once led a school that decided upon: 'Success for All' – simple and concise.

In forming the mission statement, you might be best advised to first agree principles rather than get hung up on wording. The latter best done by a small group of people at a later stage.

You will be surprised upon the degree of consensus that will emerge. Most of your staff will aim for the centre ground – they will avoid extremes.

For illustrative purposes, I offer two mission statements for schools that I have led. They are very different. Yours will be different again.

For a non-denominational school

We aim to provide all of our pupils with meaningful experiences in each area of school life. We strive for excellent standards and have high expectations for each of the children in our care. We are open with children and parents/guardians about the progress that is being made; the cornerstone of all that we do must be effective teaching. We see the quality of our staff as crucial to the future success of our pupils and we will invest in their training and development accordingly. Our school is a disciplined and caring environment where everyone has the right to feel valued.

For a faith school

We are first and foremost a Catholic school: an extension of home and parish. Christ is at the centre of all that we do. We are proud of our Catholic Faith, which is taught and 'lived out' at our school. The Gospel teachings are explored throughout our day, and time is made to talk with God. People are 'key' to our hopes. We value their diversity. We aim to ensure that each person in our school moves forward in their development as a whole person, made in the image of Christ. We want our 'people', big or small, to grow in their love of God and of one another. This is evident in our prayerful worship and joyful celebration of the liturgy. The curriculum is rich and varied. We look to develop everyone's knowledge, understanding and skills. We strive for high standards of learning and achievement: we aim for all children to reach their potential. We are open with children and parents about the progress that is being made; the cornerstone of our efforts must be high calibre teaching. We will invest in each person's future. Our school is a disciplined and caring environment where each individual has the right to feel valued for the person they are, and the person they will become.

'As I was saying, this is my vision.'

Change

Managing and leading the team through change is one of the biggest challenges you will face. Schools are constantly changing. Some older colleagues will joke that it is not worth changing because in a few years' time, we will all be asked to change back.

If your school is currently rated as good and you aspire to outstanding, it stands to reason that there is going to need to be a significant amount of change – change for the better, that is. Never forget there are two types of changes: improvements and steps backward.

People don't like change

How you handle change will be one of the biggest tests, for you as a head teacher in a primary school. We'll save the biggest till later. The great Walt Disney when asked about why his organisation was so successful, replied, 'We just keep moving forward.' So how do you keep moving forward? I believe it's all in the timing. Get the timing right then you have a chance to take colleagues with you. Yes, you are going to have to be able to articulate the benefits that change will bring, but if you are trying to introduce something when people already feel overworked and unloved (back to your emotional intelligence), your efforts will be all the harder to pull off. That's when your gut instincts come in. Know your staff. Know when they are tired – when they need a break and recognise that. If I sense my team are overstretched, I try to relieve some of the pressure – no meetings for a month is always appreciated. Never be afraid to be bold. To do what is right for your people. Give people a breather then when minds are fresher, outline the change you want to pursue. The start of any new year is the best time to identify changes and then stagger their implementation through the year. Avoid the pressure points – Christmas, test periods, report writing, lesson observation weeks – you'd be surprised how the importance of timing is underrated by some leaders in schools. Others in school will have a view on the right time to do things too. Listen to them.

Why do people resist change?

Is it that they're being awkward?

I don't think so. I have never bought into the idea that people get in the car in the morning wedded to their past for the sheer hell of it.

People fear change for good reasons:

- I won't be able to do it; I've done well to get this far;
- I don't want to lose my advantage;
- I'll have to invest more time and energy, and I'm already exhausted;
- There are others more suitable than I;
- I will end up embarrassing myself or looking silly.

It will be your job to enable people to face change with confidence. This will be a key priority.

Let me share another brief story with you about change (this story is paraphrased from 'The Examined Life' by Stephen Grosz, 2014, Vintage)

Marissa Panigrosso was working on the 84th floor of the World Trade Centre, chatting to colleagues, when the first plane hit the north tower. She was hit by a wall of heat. Her face crumpled. She did not hesitate: she made her way to the nearest emergency exit and walked from the building.

The two colleagues she had been chatting to carried on with their work. They simply stayed put and carried on as if nothing had happened. Some co-workers went into a meeting. They were all to lose their lives.

The story illustrates, with tragic consequences, how difficult people find it to come away from the accepted script.

Elsewhere, research has indicated that when a fire alarm sounds, people do not act immediately. They discuss with one another and they try to work out what is happening. They wait for the situation to become more clear – the smell of smoke or advice from someone they trust.

> **Outstanding schools lap up change! They don't sit back and take it easy. They constantly find fault with what they do. But rather than be de-motivated by their shortcomings, they see them as stepping stones to something better.**

Why is it so important that we can handle change? Well, the world is constantly changing. The Californian State University's 2007 YouTube video 'Shift Happens' tells us:
- 21-year olds have watched 20,000 hours of television, played 10,000 hours of video games and sent or received 250,000 texts or emails;
- 70% of 4-year-olds have a used a computer;
- Technical information is doubling every two years;
- The US Department of Labour estimates that teenagers will have had between 10 and 14 jobs by their 38th birthday;
- We are currently preparing children for jobs using technologies that don't yet exist in order to solve problems that we don't yet know are problems.

Speaking as a 53 year old who has had just the one 'traditional' job, the last two scare me the most. And to think the video was made over ten years ago. How much have we moved on since then?

Teachers ask the following when change is mooted.

What's in it for me?	How will we do it?
Who will help me?	What will my role be?
Who will help me?	How will we measure success?
Who will help me?	

Nobody comes to work intent on doing a bad job. I firmly believe that. If they are not doing the job that you want them to do, then it's down to you to show them what the alternative looks like. That's where coaching and mentoring for your staff come in.

> **That's something that outstanding schools do better than good schools. They know the difference between coaching and mentoring and make sure there is room in the school for both.**

In our school, we introduced 'Mentoring Mondays'. When we are at our best, they happen every fortnight. A colleague would watch an 'outstanding' colleague teach their own class, then later that Monday, the mentor and the mentee would team teach a lesson they had jointly planned to the mentee's class. Two staff could be mentored on the same day by outstanding colleagues. Start where you are. If you don't have outstanding teachers, have less strong colleagues watch your 'good' ones. There are of course budget implications. If you are to release colleagues to observe others, you are looking at cover costs. However, when the cost of an average external day's training is £300, the cost of a Mentoring Monday can be comfortably offset.

Coaching, as discussed earlier, is about more than mentoring. It's about asking more than telling. It takes longer, lasting over the course of a year (or longer) where perhaps a lesson a half-term is considered. It delves deeper. Very few teachers have a coach – at least, the school doesn't plan for them to have one, although someone may act in the role informally.

> **'consistently apply themselves to honing and developing the skills and potential of their people. I suppose it is an attitude of mind, and I have been lucky enough to belong to a company which puts a high premium on training its people continuously.'**
>
> **Sir John Harvey Jones** Trouble Shooter BBC Books
> (when talking about successful companies)

Although OFSTED no longer grade individual lessons, some teachers still like to receive such affirmation. They feel it offers a degree of clarity. You will need to agree a whole school approach based upon what works for all your staff – not just some. However, I would always avoid grading Newly Qualified Teachers, who are learning their craft and for whom such grades can be an unhelpful distraction.

Below are handy proformas for both coaching and mentoring staff.

Record of Coaching for Teacher	Half-term 1 2 3 4 5 6 (please circle)
What are the areas for improvement identified together?	• •
How can we best address these?	• •
Plan for next lesson	Date
Learning objectives	• •
Success criteria	• •
Introduction	Task
Key questions	Mini plenaries (KQ to punctuate lesson)
Plenary	
Grade (Optional)	

Record of Mentoring	Teacher...
	Date..
What did I learn through observing colleague teach?	<ul><li></li><li></li><li></li><li></li></ul>
What did I learn through teaching together?	<ul><li></li><li></li></ul>
What questions/ thoughts am I left with?	<ul><li></li><li></li></ul>
What will I do differently moving forward to move my teaching to outstanding?	<ul><li></li><li></li></ul>

Action Planning

**Outstanding schools have a plan for change,
which they shout from the roof tops!**

An action plan is more than just a plan. It's no less than a public declaration of what you intend to achieve and how you get there. At St Bede's, in 2016, we discussed together what our five aims would be for 2019 – it is important that you agree it together if you want people to buy-in – and then we published the aims and actions – in different versions for staff, governors, parents and children. Parents and children got a colour A4 'folded in three' leaflet and a business card with the five aims printed upon them. We had the aims printed large on banners that hung outside of school and inside the foyer. One colleague I coach went one step further and produced a fridge magnet for parents that identified his priorities.

Then – and this is the crucial bit – we write to parents each term for the next three years to say how we are doing. We never let stakeholders lose sight of the plan. OFSTED love some words more than others – one of their favourites is IMPACT. 'Yes, yes, yes,' they say, 'you are doing x, y and z, but what impact is that having on teaching and learning?' At our school, these *state of the nation letters* came from the Head Teacher. They could just as easily have come from the governors. Which would be stronger is a matter for discussion. They are frank. Parents say they like them for their straightforward approach. (I have reproduced one for you on the next page, to give you a flavour.)

The action plan should be seamlessly embedded into your schools self-evaluation form (SEF), which needs to be simple – no more than six sides of A4; update it each term. There are many models on the market. It needs to be concise and evaluative – keep 'description' to the essentials. Ensure that all staff have contributed to it and that it has been carefully proof read. A misplaced apostrophe or incorrect spelling will set the wrong tone. Once you have proof read it, get someone else to do the same and then you do it again.

For each Governors' meeting, the Leadership Team (as opposed to the Head Teacher alone) would produce an impact statement, which would describe the successes to date against agreed 'milestones' – another favourite word of OFSTED inspectors. Shortcomings could be identified at this point and narrative offered. New additions to the plan to reflect shifting priorities could be identified too. The milestones should be manageable. Don't let others bully you into something that you know is unrealistic. If you do, milestones will quickly become millstones.

St Bede's Catholic Primary School and Nursery

July 2016

Head Teacher's Termly Letter To Parents/ Carers

Dear Family,

It has been a good year in school.

We have enjoyed many things together: circus week, trips, author visits, sports days, an ever increasing standard of teaching, a new set of reading books for KS1, a fantastic musical production of Barnum and a successful residential trip to the Isle of Wight for Y6 children.

We are faced with three particular challenges as we move forward in 2016/7. Firstly, the teacher recruitment crisis. This shows no sign of improving, with too few newly qualified teachers emerging from college. The government has now officially recognised the scale of the problem. Different schools are handling the crisis in different ways. St Bede's has decided to invest in unqualified graduates, training them in St Bede's expectations as we go. Other schools have taken a different path where they have employed overseas trained teachers or a variety of temporary qualified staff. I realise that our approach will not suit every parent. Were we to lose pupils because of our actions, we would, of course, be very sad. We ask parents to trust us: we are convinced our approach is the right one for our children. Crucially, it gives them continuity. There are local schools where classes are having as many as nine teachers in the one year. I do not exaggerate. This is a recipe for disaster.

Secondly, the government has increased the expectations for pupils at the end of KS1 and KS2. This has seen the percentage of children who pass the government tests fall both nationwide and here at St Bede's. If we are to increase standards in future years, we will need more parental support. There is a particular problem in reading. Too many of St Bede's children are not reading properly with an adult at home. When we question this, we are told that parents are too busy. If this remains the case, we will not be able to raise the number of children passing the exams – and as a consequence many will not be secondary school ready. We all need to be clear that if a child goes to secondary school not reading well, they will quickly become lost in the system. Secondary school teachers do not chase parents who don't read with their children; secondary school teachers do not listen to children read; secondary school teachers do not 'teach' children to read, period. All these things are expected to happen in the primary school. Without the ability to read well, every other lesson is a closed book – quite literally. Children can't access maths or science or design classes, if they can't read well.

The final challenge to us is academy status. This changes the way a school is run. It is taken out of local authority control and run along the lines of a business. There is pressure from different voices for our school to become an academy. The governors of St. Bede's will have to decide the next steps for our school carefully. Bishop Alan is asking all Catholic schools in the diocese to band together next autumn so that they can – if the time comes – quickly convert to multi-academy trusts. (A multi-academy trust (MAT) is a group of academies who run with one executive head teacher and one board of governors.) This would have implications for how St Bede's is managed and run in the future.

Assuring you of my best intentions

Gary Nott

Executive Head Teacher

The Detail of Improvement Plans

Such plans need to be sharp and succinct. It must be clear from the plan who will monitor and who will evaluate – two quite separate things. There are as many different styles of planning as there are plans. I reproduce two pages from one of mine on pages 64-65 so you can see how mine compares with yours. How does it differ? Where is yours better? What are the strengths of the one I offer? One thing that must be clear: your objectives should be what you are going to do, not the outcomes that will result from your actions – outcomes belong in the success criteria box.

All of the action plans I write, start with five commitments from me to parents (see letter on page 63). In this way they can hold me to account and I am seen to put myself on the line. They like that, they tell me.

In terms of timings, I would advocate a three year plan. Stalin and I both tried five year plans, and they don't work. Five years is an age. But if you try to see where you want to be in three years' time and then work yourself backwards – setting interim goals for the end of Y1 and Y2 and then planning actions in detail for Y1 – you will have a wider perspective.

8

Activity Eight
Where do you see your school in three years' time? Could you describe that in five pithy SMART targets? If not, you don't know your school well enough yet or indeed where you want to be. Don't think they have to be set in stone. You can amend them a little, as you go. Start with the previous head teacher's SEF and the last OFSTED report — the latter is always a good starting point. After all, it will be where your next inspection team start.

St Bede's Catholic Primary School and Nursery

September 2015

5 Commitments

Dear Family,

We are delighted to be leading the school on a path to excellence. We are making many changes, which our dynamic team are implementing consistently, across the school. There are ten aims to our plan for this year and we will be working hard to deliver all ten. We have selected five aims to commit to publicly for parents, our primary stakeholders.

By July 2016, we will ensure that:

- the percentage of children gaining higher levels of attainment at age 7 will be higher
- all teaching will be good or better
- more children will make good progress in their maths
- fewer good staff will leave the school
- behaviour in the school will be 'outstanding'.

Gary Nott
Executive Head Teacher

Strand: Effectiveness of Leadership and Management

Aim 1: To make our leaders' performance 'outstanding' so that teaching and learning are improved.

Key Success Criterion: leaders can evidence how they have impacted upon raising standards of teaching and learning (see subject audits and staff performance management 'impact' statements)

Objectives	Steps	Lead	Timings/Cost	Leaders' Monitoring Process: Are the actions being completed?	Success Criteria: Have the actions had the desired effect?	Milestones
Senior and middle leaders can ensure the conditions are right for people to lead and manage effectively. Leaders can make paperwork more coherent and streamlined	Work alongside an outstanding school, St Bede's, in order to develop leadership and Management at Farnham Green.	GN CJ and SLTs and English and Maths managers	2015/6	Are colleagues from the partner school timetabled to work alongside FG Assistant Heads? English and Maths managers? Their reports to be evidenced in the HT's report to both governing bodies.	More opportunities for middle and senior leaders to lead; they should be able to evidence through their subject audit how they have impacted upon the quality of teaching and learning.	January 31st: Subject audits published. St Bede's Impact Logs to be available for inspection.
	Specifically, to involve the St Bede's LT in improving the quality of leadership through: coaching mentoring INSET.	Friday AM visits to Y2 and EYFS from St Bede's assistant heads	EYFS and Y1/2 to begin in autumn 2 spring 1 Y3/4		Senior leaders given greater opportunities to impact upon progress within their phase – see Performance Management Documents 'Impact Statements'.	Termly observations of teaching, work and planning scrutinies (see performance management plans).
	Introduce pupil flight plans and class cockpits in order to track pupil performance.	GN	Spring 1	Published to all teaching staff		Autumn: 75% of 'teaching' judged good + Spring 90% of 'teaching' judged good +

Strand: Effectiveness of Leadership and Management

Aim 1: To make our leaders' performance 'outstanding' so that teaching and learning are improved.

Key Success Criterion: leaders can evidence how they have impacted upon raising standards of teaching and learning (see subject audits and staff performance management 'impact' statements)

Objectives	Steps	Lead	Timings/Cost	Leaders' Monitoring Process: Are the actions being completed?	Success Criteria: Have the actions had the desired effect?	Milestones
	Introduce coherent arrangements for Performance Management – triangulation!	GN	Lesson observations and book and planning scrutinies in: autumn 1; spring 1; and summer 1 progress reviews – spring 1 and summer 1 and summer 2	Published to all teaching staff	The team at FG say the leaders of the school support them exceptionally well in their efforts and this makes teaching easier	Summer Term: 100% of 'teaching' judged good+ May questionnaire Class/ Set Flight Plans and Cockpits published in January, April and June Termly progress meetings with phase and performance management leaders January, April and June

Monitoring versus Evaluation and Efficiency versus Effectiveness

Activity Nine
Which is it better to be: efficient or effective?
You can, in this scenario, only be one.
Give it some thought then read on.

Yes, those of you who chose effective get the prize. There is no point in being efficient if you aren't having the desired effect.

OFSTED are quick to say yes, I can see you have done x, y and z – and you may have done them well – but (and this is the killer), 'So what?'

And then there's monitoring versus evaluation
Monitoring is a relatively low level activity. All sorts of people can monitor. You don't have to be a head teacher to do it. Give someone a metaphorical clipboard and they are away. You would be surprised at how much of their term a new Head teacher is tempted to spend monitoring. It makes them feel useful because they are busy. But it doesn't mean they are being effective. Evaluation, by contrast, is one of the hardest things we do in school. It involves the 'i' word – yes, you guessed it impact. HMIs like to talk about impact – 'Yes,' they say, 'that's lovely, but how have you judged the impact?' We spend far less time evaluating than we do monitoring, when the reverse should be true.

To judge impact (to evaluate) you need to identify what success will look like. Truly SMART (Specific, Measurable, Achievable, Realistic and Time Related) objectives don't usually need additional performance indicators (statements by which you will judge success); they are already contained within the objective.

For example:
To improve children's mental ability strategies so that 80% of children score 14/20+ in the June tests.

"I am busy monitoring so I must be earning my money, right?"

OFSTED

I currently lead an outstanding school. I say currently, because nothing stands still. Some of you may have been judged to be outstanding in the past – only to be stamped good this latest time around. Who knows what the future holds for my own school? We can but try our best. When I went to the school as head teacher in September 2012, it had by the former head's admission dropped from an outstanding school in 2008 to a good one with some outstanding features; in my judgement she was being over generous – forgivable, being close to her retirement – rose coloured spectacles and all that! There was nothing that warranted the outstanding label, in my view. Good yes, solid good in some instances, outstanding, no. It's a long haul from good to outstanding. How did we do it in a relatively short space of time? In a word: teamwork. This outstanding teamwork led to outstanding data. You can't be outstanding without the data! But having the data is no guarantee of being outstanding. It's quite a conundrum! In this book, I try to give you a flavour of what we did in our journey, which took just over two years.

However, I don't want to write about outstanding schools. I want to write about outstanding primary schools. If the school isn't outstanding in its delivery of a primary education – in its fullest sense – then the job hasn't been done. Never lose sight of that: it stretches from how we teach PSHE to science, to English and maths.

Where to start?

First, motivation, again.

10 | **Activity Ten**
Why do you want to be judged outstanding?
List the reasons.

It's not about external accreditation. Or at least, it shouldn't be.

The work of an inspector is relatively simple. Despite their protestations to the contrary, they risk very little but hold enormous sway over the people whom they judge. Inspectors don't create, you do. The criticisms they produce can

be self-satisfying to record – dare we even say amusing? – but can do untold damage to your team's aspirations and confidence. In recent years, we have all become consumed with chasing the 'outstanding' label and this is unhelpful. It is a distraction. Even the new Chief Executive of OFSTED at the time of writing has talked about doing away with the term. You are where you are and, for now, good may need to be good enough.

You must see OFSTED for what it is. Give it respect, yes but do not allow it to have undue prominence in your mind or you will transmit this to staff. If it does, you will always be chasing shadows. It cannot be 'the' means to 'the' end. A 'successful' school should be what you strive for. And, you do it for the staff and pupils who make up the school. Praise from OFSTED should simply be the icing on the cake – no more than that.

It's about delivering excellence.

'We judge our own worth.' Or at least we should.

> ### And outstanding schools do: they don't need OFSTED to tell them what they already know.

If OFSTED disappeared tomorrow, unlikely unless the Green Party should be elected (the only party to feature such a commitment in their last manifesto), then we would still want excellence for our children. Wouldn't we?

But I think it's worth asking the question because if all you're looking for is a recipe that will work for all of you to get you the accolade –'outstanding' – you will be falling at the first post. If it was that easy, everyone would be doing it. By 'it', I mean exactly the same thing.

OFSTED don't want that.

And that, in my view, is the first lesson.
OFSTED want schools that innovate! Do things differently.

So what do you do at your school that you are confident the school down the road isn't replicating? Something that is unique.

Activity Eleven
List two things that are unique about your school...
Did you struggle?   Do you even know one?

To innovate you need creative minds and people prepared to take risks.

Why don't people take risks anymore? They used to, in the 70s and 80s – it was called *the school improvement movement*.

The Flea Circus analogy is useful here.

Some fascinating facts about flea circuses for your entertainment:

 Fleas can be 'trained' to do all sorts of things in a miniature circus. The first challenge for the adroit trainer is to establish for which act the flea has an aptitude. Once allocated a task in the show, they are fitted with a harness. Yes, really! A delicate wire is wrapped around their neck and when attached to items larger than the flea, hey presto, we have a moving object! Fleas that like to run can spin a carousel, pull small wagons or even race against one another. Elsewhere, fleas that like to jump can be 'trained' to kick balls – they will jump 'away' and hit the ball when so doing. The flea really is a talented little chap!

But the important point I want to make here is about why people don't take risks anymore and performing fleas can help. Fleas can jump 10cm in the air. However, if you put them in a cup that is 5cm high, then cover the cup with a piece of card, the flea will spend some time hitting his head. When you eventually take the card away – after some considerable time, I might add, the flea will continue to jump just the 5cm – no more, even though they are inherently capable. No fleas, I hasten to add, were harmed in the making of this discovery!

Assessment levels are one area where our school chose to take risks and do things differently.

We have had attainment levels for over twenty years. Successive politicians have argued for them. Now we are told we are not to have them anymore. But why? The educational arguments seem more than a little bit flimsy to me. We are told that they are too broad, but anything the government now comes up with won't be more sophisticated than 3c to 6c – that's ten steps – the government is proposing a 10 grade attainment scale at Y6. Where's the difference?

What do your parents think? Do you know?

One of the key roles of your school is to reflect the views of stakeholders – in this case, staff and parents.

We asked our parents what they thought.

They said:

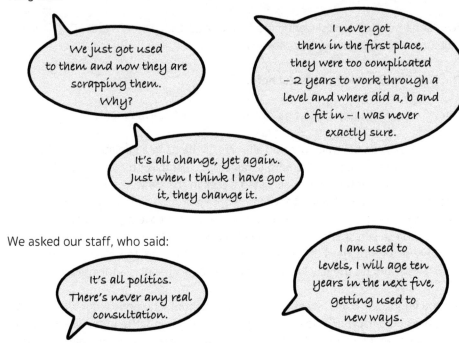

We just got used to them and now they are scrapping them. Why?

I never got them in the first place, they were too complicated – 2 years to work through a level and where did a, b and c fit in – I was never exactly sure.

It's all change, yet again. Just when I think I have got it, they change it.

We asked our staff, who said:

It's all politics. There's never any real consultation.

I am used to levels, I will age ten years in the next five, getting used to new ways.

So, we, and I mean 'we' (staff and governors – as a team), decided to stick with levels. But to change them just a little. Instead of taking two years to pass through a band, we decided that one year would be more accessible to parents:

So Y1 would comprise level 1 – 1c, 1b and 1a.

1c, not meeting expectations; 1a, exceeding them.

We decided that gifted and talented pupils could be placed out of year, as could special needs children. So a particularly bright child in Y4 could be a 5b.

A struggling pupil in Y3 could be a 2b.

It's not perfect. But it is us thinking on our feet, having listened to parents and staff.

When we outlined the plans to OFSTED in 2015, they said, 'Haven't heard of that yet – makes sense.' We didn't like to claim innovation in this regard, because we thought lots of other people would be doing likewise. 'They weren't,' said OFSTED.

Am I recommending you do what we did? No. It appears right for us; it may not be for you. What I am recommending is that you think outside the box. It's a way of moving from good to outstanding. Jump higher!

> **An outstanding school is one that innovates! Get that word, innovative, into your report and you will be on your way.**

That said, there are approaches that all schools can learn from. Take from them what suits your circumstances – ie, apply some judgement.

Moving an OFSTED Grade

I have heard it said that it is harder to move from 'good' to 'outstanding' than it is from 'requires improvement' to 'good'. I am undecided. Certainly, the harder slog and the more stressful climb, was the latter. Working in a school that requires improvement is no fun. Everything is doubly hard. Class observations, book and planning scrutinies tend to be half-termly rather than termly. Pupil progress reviews tend to be more frequent – though hopefully not every three weeks as was reported to me by one local school. Staff are under constant scrutiny. I think the assistance of an executive head from a neighbouring local school can be vital to ensuring success. You need that wider perspective that comes with experience of what has been needed to achieve the outstanding accolade: such an executive head – if they are worth their salt – will be able to point to quick gains with a fresh pair of eyes. And, often it is no more complicated than that. Not all incumbent heads will welcome such support, however. It calls for a certain degree of humility and self-sacrifice and for many heads can be a bitter pill to swallow – understandably so. It could be argued that for schools that find themselves in such circumstances, a change in leadership is the only way forward. Whilst I would agree that may be the case for schools judged 'inadequate', I think there is plenty of life left in the typical head who finds their school banded one that requires improvement. After all, it can happen to us all. All it takes in the current system is one bad set of results at the wrong time – inspection time. As my doctor said to me recently – referring to an impending blood test – you are only as good as your last set of results.

Moving from good to outstanding is about all the small things that I have tried to highlight in this book. But make no mistake, data will be key. If the practice supports the outstanding data you are home and dry; however, if the practice doesn't support the outstanding data, you still won't make it over the finish line – inspectors will not be able to conclude that the impressive results are down to what you are doing – maybe you just have able pupils and teaching that is no better than 'good'.

Handling Inspections

As a Head Teacher or Executive Head Teacher, I have had ten OFSTED inspections. I say have 'had' because I am struggling to think of a more exciting word – endured, enjoyed; there is no one word that captures my feelings to them as a whole.

On balance, I think the more inspections you have, the less phased you are by them. But it doesn't matter how long you have been a head teacher, the feeling of dread never goes completely and it won't change because you may now be 'treated' to a light touch one day scrutiny – at the back of your mind will be the full inspection that would be triggered should the one day not go well. Even light touch inspections can be expected to feature the usual ingredients: meetings with you in your role as head teacher, the deputy or assistant head teachers and middle leaders; meetings with members of the governing body; discussions with a representative from the local authority (or MAT); hearing pupils read from Years 1 to 6; the scrutiny of statutory test data and the school's own data; the scrutiny of school documents, including safeguarding records, policies and procedures, the single central record of pre-employment checks, and assessment information; visits to lessons across the school with the head teacher; a scrutiny of a range of pupils' books with the head teacher and the deputy head teacher; informal discussions with parents at the start of the school day; consideration of parent responses to Parent View. There might not be time for the School Council (there may), but most other things will continue to feature. And the fact that they are even briefer snapshots than what is seen in a two day inspection will mean that you won't get as much time to challenge misconceptions.

I certainly enjoyed the inspections that went well. They were almost pleasurable. When things are going well, even luck seems to be on your side and the cards can fall neatly into place.

Along the way I had two 'rogue' teams. Those inspections I endured. They taught me that lead inspectors are just people and like all people they can get it wrong. In such circumstances, it is crucial that you battle tenaciously for control of the inspection. Unless you are successful, you will be on a hiding to nothing and your fate will be sealed until you get another opportunity to prove yourself next time round. It can be a long resentful wait.

Such a battle begins from the first phone call. If the inspector is spinning a narrative with which you disagree, you must say so. This feels awkward. You want to be deferential, for fear of getting on the lead inspector's wrong side so early on. But viewpoints are quickly formed in an OFTSED inspection, whatever the Chief Inspector of Schools may say to the contrary. The inspection team has to work with speed and will have come to their tentative conclusions by the end of the first morning. Then they set about testing them.

So that first phone call. Have your key messages written on one side of A4. This is time for the broken record scenario – repeat your key messages over and over. Be prepared to back them up with a concise reference to the latest data. The inspector may not have it. Their hypothesis may be out of date, resting all too often on last year's data. Remember, you know your school better than they. Be brave, after all they have yet to step foot in it. What they think they know is ready to be challenged.

During the inspection you will want your school to be at its best. I would resist the temptation to give the children a pep talk. I prefer to keep it natural, letting the inspector or inspectors see the children as they would normally be. However, the whole staff need a briefing from you at the start of the inspection and midway through. The initial meeting will give you an opportunity to make sure key messages are concisely delivered. If you have prepared them properly, this will be a summary of messages with which they are very familiar – having heard them time and time again. The inspection team will in turn tell you where they are at the end of the first day. If they need to see something in Day 2, for example greater challenge, a fair team will tell you. You then need to tell your staff before they leave for the evening what inspectors will be looking for in Day 2 – they can literally sleep on it.

Following the inspection, you will be sent the draft report for comment. You will be told that only factual inaccuracies will be considered for change. But most inspectors will entertain other changes too, although not changes to summative judgements. You need to think carefully and quickly – you get 24 hours – as to what changes you want made. There will be many but you will need to prioritise because you can't ask for too many. It is a fine balancing act. Ask for too much and you are likely to come away empty handed. The most I have ever asked for was fifteen, of which I secured ten.

If you do find yourself in a position where you want to appeal against the decision and the judgements given, you will need the experience of your local authority to support you. The appeal must come from your Chair. Is it worth appealing? I used to think not. However, recent experience has taught me that judgements do get changed. I don't know how frequently and I would guess that more often than not they remain the same. OFSTED themselves inform you that an appeal against their findings will not usually halt the publication of a report. I think that says it all. Once a report has been published, I think you can reasonably forget it. The appeal in such cases is going nowhere; I have never seen a published report rescinded.

A final word, about OFSTED. Don't fear them. Be stronger than that. I have known capable, industrious, brilliant colleagues burst into tears when they knew OFSTED were coming. I offer the following story as a heart warmer; it is based on my own experience of ten inspection teams. It's the kind of OFSTED that I believe in.

Mr Thomas' Story (A story for grown-ups!)

Mr Thomas knew his OFSTED inspection was coming. He would glance at the clock on Wednesday at midday and think he had survived for another week. It was no way to live your working life. It was akin to walking a tight-rope – seemingly, without a net.

He had prepared his staff rather well, on balance, he thought; and on his wall could be seen an inspection 'Things To Do List' – his attempt to prepare himself! He had crossed each heading off over the past few months. The only trouble being, he now needed to revisit what was at the beginning of the list as that was now more than a little out of date.

His Tuesday morning had started badly. He had met Dianne coming out of the staff room. Dianne was one of his most experienced teachers. She was an excellent practitioner. However, she was disabled in that she suffered from episodes of manic depression. He managed her well, he thought. When she was high, her husband would attempt to stabilise her by putting tranquilisers in her morning coffee, for she had no insight into her own condition: Dianne couldn't tell if she were up or down. Inevitably, he would have to choose his moment to tell her that she wasn't well. If he judged it right, she would be compliant and let him drive her home. Some governors were uneasy with his approach, but he wasn't going to be the one to tell Dianne that she no longer had a place in his school. He wasn't built like that. He made a mental note to catch up with her later in the day, to judge her mood.

The builders had arrived early that morning; the roof of the boys' toilets in the top end of school needed to be resurfaced. It had been leaking. He wasn't sure about this particular crew, but the local authority had recommended them and he didn't have the time to hunt around for an alternative. The job was urgent. They had been experiencing bouts of heavy rain with more forecast for later that day.

In his office at lunchtime, he had just started to make headway with his post when a call was transferred to him. Janet said simply: 'It's the call you have been waiting for!'

He went cold.

Half an hour or so later, he was in possession of the key facts. They were to be inspected by a team of three, the next day and the day after. He called an impromptu meeting of staff and broke the news. They seemed okay, even Dianne – about whom he had been worried earlier on.

He didn't get much sleep that night.

In his office at 8.00 prompt the following morning, he introduced himself to the three inspectors. He was to join the lead on a tour of Y6 and Y2 classrooms first thing. Y6, he was confident about, of Y2 he was less sure. The Y6 teachers were pumped and things went well. In a short catch-up with the inspector afterwards, he was invited to say what he had liked and where there was room for further improvement. Overall, the inspector announced himself to be happy. They arrived in the first Y2 class shortly after break. The children had been asked to mime a well known idiom to their partner. Why? – was his first thought. After ten minutes or so, he could see the inspector was becoming edgy. The pace was too slow and the task questionable. He found himself trying to catch the eye of the teacher to indicate to her somehow that this wasn't working and to move on. But she wasn't looking in his direction. Although – truth be told – he wasn't exactly sure how he would get the message to her with facial antics that he would have to conceal from the inspector. But then the lead stood and they were on their way. As he had feared, the inspector was less than impressed. How he wondered were the lesson observations going in the other parts of the school?

The day ended at five, following a brief team meeting of the inspectors – to which he was not invited. As he drove home he recalled the events of the day. Things had seemed to be going well until the Y2 disappointment.

He unwound with a stiff drink. It had been raining heavily on the way home and the journey had been grim – too many thoughts swirling round in his mind. They had supper and at just gone 7.00 there was a call for him. It was Terry, the caretaker.

'You're not going to like it,' he said. 'Those flaming builders knocked off for the day leaving a ruddy great hole where the toilet roof had been.'

The caretaker relayed to him how the tarpaulin the builders had stretched over the gaping hole – where once there had been roof – had been woefully inadequate and as a consequence the cloud burst at 6.00 had seen rainwater cascade into the boy's toilets and then through the door. The main corridor, which ran from one end of the school to the other, was reported to be one long mass of soaked carpet.

He groaned.

'I'm on my way,' he said.

When he arrived at the school, the builders were on site. He resisted the urge to ask them where they had tied their horses up – for cowboys they most certainly were. He just wanted a solution to the problem.

The solution was that the carpet tiles would have to be torn up and put outside. The floors would then have to be mopped. There being no such thing as clean water, he then had to get on the phone to a local sanitiser who said he could spray the building that night and yes it would be ready for the morning but there would be a hefty bill to pay. Just do it, he had said.

He climbed into bed a little before 1.00 and was on site again just six hours later to welcome the inspectors, who were surprised to find no carpet where there had been one the day before. He had time to explain to them briefly and then they were off again. More lesson observations. He groaned inwardly when in 4P Ben Simpkins could be heard saying to one of the inspection team, 'We don't usually do this, you know!'

Just before lunch, the lead inspector knocked at his door. 'You have a teacher called Dianne Jenkins?' he said.

'Yes, that's right,' he mumbled. Dianne! He hadn't given her a second thought since Tuesday.

'I think she may be unwell.'

'Unwell?'

Yes unwell. Her teaching assistant is with the class so they are fine but Mrs Jenkins is, I am afraid, lying down in the book corner.'

He dropped Dianne off at home. She had agreed that she was unwell.

There was nothing to be done. It was one of those things. He returned to school with a heavy heart and at 4.00 was ushered into the inspection team's debriefing for the day.

He feared the worse.

'Well,' said the lead inspector, his face inscrutable, 'it has been an interesting two days.' "*Interesting*", he thought. Not quite the word he would have used.

The inspector continued. 'Not only have you had an inspection to deal with,' – where was this going? he thought – 'but a flood and a teacher who became so incapacitated that they could not continue with their class.'

His head dropped and his shoulders sunk.

This was going to be bad. Worse than he had feared,

'We saw good teaching with just a few exceptions. You managed to cope admirably with the water egress to the school – most importantly, you didn't have to shut – and through your careful people management, a talented teacher who suffers with a disability is kept on board your bus for the most part and, when she is unwell, you deal with it. In short, we like what we see. Well done!'

As he drove home that evening he realised that Dianne's illness and the errant builders' flood had been the making of the inspection, not his downfall. Who would have thought it? These OFSTED people could be fair, after all. It made him want to write about his experience. But who would believe it?

Cause and Effect

Some interesting work has recently been done by the Education Endowment Foundation into the relative impact of different variables within a school. I present it for you below. The impact of different approaches on learning are listed in rank order – most impact to least.

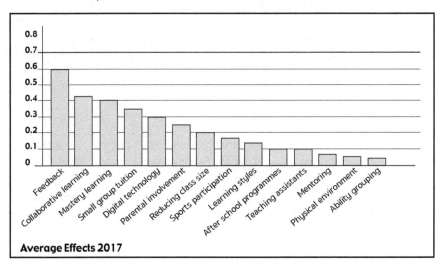

Average Effects 2017

Research is of course invaluable in widening our perspectives. Based on my own experience, I would nevertheless reorganise the order thus:

1st	Feedback
2nd	Ability grouping*
3rd	Small group tuition
4th	After school programmes
5th	Collaborative learning
6th	Parental involvement
7th	Teaching assistants
8th	Mentoring
9th	Reducing class size
10th	Mastery Learning
11th	Digital technology
12th	Learning styles
13th	Physical environment
14th	Sports participation

Activity Twelve
Based on your own experience, where would you place the bars on the chart? What does this say about you and the school you will run?

Outstanding schools don't just accept what the research is telling them. They reflect upon their own experience and context.

I don't see a contradiction between having mastery learning and ability sets in my top ten. But this would depend upon your definition of mastery. For me it means only that learning is deep and not superficial – that learners can apply their knowledge in a range of contexts; they are thinking about what they have learned and how they have learned it; and they know what progress they are making. I do not subscribe to the idea that some colleagues hold that it necessarily means mixed ability classes needing to be kept together, only moving on when the vast majority of children – if not all children – have acquired the particular skill set or body of knowledge. But my list doesn't matter, neither does my definition of mastery – yours do. You must have a rationale for why you have placed things above others. Such decisions will shape your headship.

* Crucially my model of ability grouping centres upon reducing the size of the lowest attaining groups and assigning high-performing teachers to these groups with additional targeted catch up support.

Every Day Matters

The emphasis upon attendance has shot through the roof in the last decade. Those of us who teach, know that every day counts – so much is crammed into the one day! But explain that to the average parent, who hears 91% and thinks that is job done!

I list for you some tried and tested approaches:

- a termly report card that indicates amongst other things (conduct, effort, progress) whether attendance is above, below or in line with national averages;
  or a RAG system of termly letters for parents – green paper for above, you get the idea...;
- trophies for best class;
- rewards for 100% attendees;
- a zero-tolerance approach to term-time holidays;
- appointments outside of school time;
- a detailed analysis of how attendance was affected in weeks that included religious observance or bouts of illness.

There is nothing new about much of this. However, for persistent absentees (those whose attendance falls below 90%), I would suggest you can't beat an insistence upon seeing medical evidence before further absence is authorised; once, that is, we hit October half-term. Before that point, just four days missed can see you labelled a persistent absentee. Being unfairly labelled after seven weeks of school will only serve to antagonise parents!

"Come on Mrs Jenkins, own up; we know you were away in Tenerife!"

Section 5: Your Team

Your Bus

It became topical some while back to talk about buses in educational circles. It was time, some said, to bite the bullet and get some people off your bus. By people, I think what was meant was the 'blockers' to use current terminology, the awkward squad – those people who were going to resist the change you wanted to bring about.

Having intervened in the running of three schools that were underperforming, it can certainly be the case that you may inherit some people who at first sight seem determined to work against you. You are the driver of the bus. That is not in doubt. However, it may well be that the way in which the bus was driven in the past has resulted in these so called difficult people adopting the attitudes with which they now present. Maybe the bus was driven too quickly or the corners taken too sharply. You will want to reassure people in your first few weeks that, if that has been the case, things will be different with the change of driver. That doesn't mean a joy ride but it does mean acknowledging that some of your blockers will have been on the bus for some time – for far longer than you. It is your job to keep them on board, not off load them at the first opportunity.

If you inherit a school that needs to see some rapid improvements, the real challenge is to achieve them with the same people on the bus. You are not a premier league football manager taking up the reins of a new post and selling all those players who don't immediately fit your ideology of what you think they should look like. Any head worth their salt can bring about improvements with new people they have been able to select. The challenges and rewards come with achieving things with other people's appointments.

So resist the temptation in your first few months to identify those people who you want to alight at the next stop – work with the cards you have been dealt. The blockers will pick up on the fact that you are not discarding them and, once they feel wanted, they may well warm to the task in hand and to you.

Your Deputy

Your relationship with your deputy is one of the most crucial ones. Before you start working together, take them out to lunch – always a good start. Take an interest in them as people. Find out about their family, motivation and aspirations. Let them know that you will be there to support them in all that they do. Ask that they support you in public but make sure they understand they can disagree with you in private. Make explicit to them that they must tell you as soon as they feel unhappy with any aspect of your relationship. You can't mend things if you are not aware of any difficulties that arise – and arise they might. The relationship is like a good marriage; it has to be worked at. Communication is key. Make sure they have an understanding of how you like to work – you don't want your actions in the early days to be misinterpreted when you are just getting to know one another. And, if they applied for your job, things are going to be difficult. I have known, in such circumstances, only a parting of company to fix things with any real degree of satisfaction.

When appointed as a new head teacher, you must not make the mistake of feeling threatened by an already established deputy, especially if they have been in the school for some considerable time. Let them shine. Be prepared to show staff that you are prepared to defer to them in some circumstances given their better knowledge of the school. The better they are at their job, the more effective your school will be. This can be a complicated manoeuvre because you want to establish yourself as the head teacher. Don't lose sight of the fact that it is a double act, not a one (wo)man show.

Your deputy in a primary school is going to need to be both an effective leader and manager. I say both because the model of deputy headship that I welcome is not the one that I inherited some years ago when I myself became a deputy. In those far off times, the deputy was a glorified teacher who acted as a conduit for the staff's dissatisfaction to the head teacher and who deputised for the head when they were out. Some of your older staff will remember this role and still see your deputy in this way, if you let them. The modern incarnation of a deputy head teacher places him or her firmly alongside the head, not below her or him in some outdated hierarchical model. Rather, sharing the management and leadership of the school, as a kind of 'associate' head teacher. On a day-to-day basis, decisions are thus shared and leadership and management are joined. Nick Butt, OFSTED inspector, argues that as deputy you will need to come up with some initiatives of your own and see them through: stake out your claim to individuality. I prefer to see that as a number of shared initiatives that you will see through together with the Head – their priorities should be yours – their initiatives, in part, yours. That may even mean ultimately delegating the execution of the idea to another leader within the school, but this is something you will be 'seen' to be doing together.

Indeed, I would argue for more. You are really working well together when the whole leadership team is seen as one voice – one entity taking decisions together for the benefit of the wider good. Not just the Head together with their deputy, or associate – whichever you prefer to call them. In fact, next year, in my own school, I am dispensing with the deputy role because I want the role shared more explicitly – in the first instance, between four assistant head teachers. By removing the more expensive deputy post, I can afford to have more than one assistant. You can only realistically do this when your existing deputy leaves. A restructuring would leave any existing deputy understandably feeling undermined if demoted. You should be aware, however, that contractually there are a few things that the assistant cannot do. Only a deputy (in the Head's absence) can exclude a child, for example.

And Assistant Head is a much better title for the distributed leadership 'associate' that I am proposing. It is ironic that the powers that be created the assistant head role, but at a level below that of deputy. I think they missed a trick .The deputy that I am talking about does not merely deputise for the Head when she or he is out (although they would), but they assist the Head when she or he is in. The difference is clear to see. And to make their role credible, the Head must be prepared to defer to them from time to time in decision making when she or he is not part of the consensus. They must be given a chance to lead, even when the Head thinks it might be a risk – against, as it were, their better judgement.

I used to think that the only deputy worth having was one who aspired to headship. But over the years I have met several effective deputies who did not want to take things that far in their career. I think this has become a more credible stance to adopt as the role of deputy as a leader and manger in their own right has flourished – it has become a role with teeth. However, beware the non-teaching deputy. In my experience they lack credibility with the staff. Some staff will wonder what they do with their time. You may know, but perception is key. Your deputy should be one of your very best teachers and should therefore be based in the classroom (preferably in a year group that is statutorily assessed); albeit with significant release time so they can assist you in the running of the school.

13	**Activity Thirteen** How might a Head demonstrate to the staff that this is in all but name an equal partnership — that he has an associate?

The Subject Leader

Subject leaders have a difficult job in schools. They are handed lots of responsibilities without many rights. Ultimately, in some schools, it is the Head or deputy who will decide where a particular path is to be trod, not them. I have tried to instil in my subject leaders that they are in charge of their area: I, like other colleagues, expect to be consulted on initiatives but at the end of the day, the subject leader decides how we will proceed. They should be at the centre of decision making in their area – all key decisions should be led by them. Inevitably they, like you, will need to lead by consensus but they must feel empowered. I like to say to my subject leaders, 'Well what do you want to do? It is your subject area, after all.' The buck may well stop with me, but it is their call.

The subject policy should be short, pithy and well known. It should not be gathering dust somewhere. It should reflect what is happening in class. Ideally, it should be no more than two sides of A4.

I encourage my subject leaders to keep a running audit of their subject as we proceed through the year. In it I expect them to make judgements about lessons observed, books scrutinised and the planning that they have analysed. They should also be talking to pupils about the delivery of their subject.

You will need to invest in your subject leaders. Core leaders will need an injection of time away from classroom responsibilities and all subject leaders will need release to observe teaching and learning. You will need to manage subject priorities well or funds will be short and teachers will feel overwhelmed at too broad a scrutiny. In my view, there should be no more than one observation per term for a good teacher; although learning walks at other times can complement such opportunities. In small schools, the head and deputy must be prepared to soak up more than one curriculum area to lead if the few other staff are to be treated fairly. External training opportunities are expensive. Much can be learned by allowing subject leaders from a group of schools to meet together to share experiences. I have found a handbook for subject leaders to be invaluable – it should state how the role is to be carried through at the school you lead. Don't aim to develop every subject every year, you won't have the time or resources, notably money. Prioritise!

A subject leader audit should answer the following questions:

- Are people clear on the policy?
- Which parts of the policy are being delivered well?
- Which parts, not so well?
- Do we need to make changes to the policy or do people need to be further encouraged to do what is already being asked of them?
- Is the scheme of work doing what we want it to?
- Where could we improve it?
- Do we have the resources to do that?
- What standards are being achieved in the subject? Are they in line with national expectations, or do they exceed them? How do we know?
- Have recent changes in the subject had the desired impact? How do we know?
- Can children describe what they have been learning in the subject?
- Do children enjoy the subject? Why? Why not?

'Yes, but why do you say that you don't enjoy history as much as PE?'

Governors

'...believe that anything is possible when you have the right people to support you.'

Misty Copeland (Ballet Dancer)

A while back governors were asked to be 'critical friends'.

I have never liked that phrase.

I don't have critical friends. I have friends; if they are critical of me, they don't stay friends for very long. Loving, caring, funny, optimistic, reassuring – all adjectives I would put in front of the noun friend – but critical, no.

The whole thing smacks of a relationship that I don't want.

Can you imagine the board of directors of Esso describing themselves as critical friends of the CEO?

Don't misunderstand me; many of my governors have become friends over the years – but outside of their role of governance. Being a governor is a 'professional' role – it just happens to be one that doesn't reward people financially. Not that there aren't rewards. There are. They come from seeing children given every chance in life to fulfil their potential. A pithy statement. One that is often said, but none the less true for that. If a governor hasn't seen an individual child reaching their potential in the last 12 months, then I am not quite sure why s/he does what they do.

Never be defensive when governors challenge you. That is what they are there to do.

How would you characterise their style currently? Does it make you want to do a better job? If not, then how might you change it? Honesty has to be your starting point. You are in this together. Have some frank, 'grown-up' conversations and set out what your expectations of them are. Be prepared though to listen to their expectations of you and the school: then together agree an approach built upon consensus.

It is a great idea for governors to send their own termly newsletter to parents. In it, they can describe what has been happening in school from their own perspective, which should chime with yours. Some governors hold termly surgeries too, when parents can come to them with things that are troubling them or suggestions they want to make – it needs to be handled carefully. Governors must be clear that it is not an opportunity to come and raise complaints with them before they have been raised with you. Your school should have a complaints procedure and governor surgeries should not circumvent it.

Recently, my own Chair of Governors has begun to produce his own termly report. It lists all the actions he has taken and clarifies how many hours he has spent in school, on emails and dealing with other correspondence. I think it adds something to the pot.

Never, never upset a governor. I have, and have lived to regret it. Bite your tongue and come back to the situation another day when minds are fresher and tempers calmer. If you take them on, you will lose even if you win!

First Appointments – Promote From Within (where you can!)

> 'I appointed someone because, between two equally strong interviewees, she presented as the candidate with a wonderfully dry sense of humour. She spent the next two years without making anyone laugh – or laughing herself for that matter.'
>
> **Head teacher**

It is probably not legal to speak in such terms. I do not want to be taken literally but I do want to try to point out the pitfalls that exist when appointing new staff from outside your school – especially for senior posts. How can you ensure that the person you are appointing is the one you think you are getting? There are a number of hurdles someone can be made to jump:

- an application form
- a supporting statement
- a task
- an interview
- a reference.

When I was appointed to my second headship, I had to:

- lead an assembly
- write a letter of introduction to the parents
- give a presentation on a theme given to me on the day
- analyse some data
- deal with a matter waiting in my in-tray (an allegation of bullying)
- meet a gathering of staff (who were all judging me!).

And still the governors told me at the end of a two day process, that they went home praying the person they thought I appeared was the person I would turn out to be.

I have appointed people on the basis of sparkling interviews where they failed to dazzle once in post. Elsewhere, I have appointed people on the basis of glowing references, which in reality turned out not to be worth the paper they were printed on.

Appointing new staff is a lottery. If you have an internal candidate with whom you have worked closely for some time, you will know what you are getting. This is not to be discounted easily. Indeed, I have worked with colleagues who have confided that given a choice, they would never appoint an 'external' deputy again, so important is the role and so hard is it to know what you are getting when appointing from outside

Outstanding schools have a proven track record of growing their own!

Interviewing Techniques
Some Dos and Don'ts

References

In the world of education, we are slightly unusual in that we tend to call for references before interviews. Despite the temptation, don't look at them before you interview. If you do you will be depriving yourself of the opportunity to interview an applicant objectively. A reference can cloud your thoughts and, particularly if it is good, the interview is in danger of becoming a self-fulfilling prophecy. You will see what you want to see – hear what you want to hear. This is a danger having read a letter of application, let alone someone else's opinions. The best interviews are done cold.

Interviews

You want examples. You don't just want to be told that someone is a creative thinker or a good problem solver. What is that worth? The person you are interviewing is unlikely to say they aren't good at such things. You want them to illustrate why they should be thought of as strong in this field. No examples – which stand probing and prodding – are a clear indicator that this person is not for you.

First Impressions

They count. The candidate will only get one chance to make one. Experience has taught me that if someone's first impression is bad, there is a strong possibility that they are not the person for you.

Social Media

If employing someone young especially, it is worth searching the Internet to see what social media accounts they hold and what they do with them. The teaching standards require colleagues to uphold the professional standards both in and out of work. It never ceases to amaze me what people – especially young people – think it is acceptable to say or post on their social networking sites. Sure as eggs is eggs, your parents and Y6 boys will search for them once they are under your employ. Be warned.

Written Statements

Any indication of poor grammar or spelling is inexcusable. It doesn't matter how positive the interview and references are. Period.

Qualifications

These are important. The fact that someone has great grades means they might be the person for you or they might not. But poor grades mean they are not.

Red Flags

Ignore them at your peril. Trust your gut. If the candidate says something that disappoints you, don't try to smooth over it and 'make it right' in your mind. There are three classic red flags:

1. Asking the question: "If you are offered the post today, will you accept it?"

Answer: "It depends: I have another interview tomorrow and I would like to know all the options available to me before deciding. After all, it's such an important decision."

Offers of employment are like marriage proposals!

Red Flag: It is bad form to say you are open to better offers. Is this a match made in heaven or not?

2. A Gap in Employment that is not accounted for.

Red Flag:
Regardless of the safer recruitment concerns – which are significant – this doesn't say, 'Employ me!'

3. Too Confident/ Over Familiarity/ Inappropriate Dress (Either sex)
Confidence is a great thing. But ...

Red Flag:
... too much confidence is a *red flag*.

You want the right mix of nerves, humility and confidence at an interview. It is a big ask but if someone gets one of the sides of the triangle out of proportion, then there is more than a suggestion that things may go wrong.

4. Late for The Interview
Red Flag:
They may be late for the job.

Take Your Time

An offer of employment – even verbal – is binding. There is no rewind button, ordinarily. Once you commit, you are stuck. This is daunting enough in the private sector but in the public sector it is awesome. In teaching, it is very difficult to terminate someone's employment. It is a marriage that will usually only end in divorce when the other party calls it a day, not you. If in doubt, sleep on it. If still in doubt, don't proceed. It is better to live and tell the tale.

Performance Management

Leading your primary school, you will be involved in managing colleagues' performance.

Outstanding schools triangulate teacher's performance.

In our school we use the following model:

My Appraisal Summary

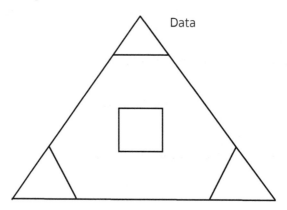

Data

Planning/ Work Scrutiny   Lesson Observations

(1 outstanding   2 good   3 Requires improvement   4 Disappointing)

Each corner of the triangle is given a grade that reflects the judgements and evidence that have been collected during the year. The overall judgement box in the middle however is the factor that decides whether the colleague will receive a pay increment that year. Data is a limiting judgement: you can't score higher than the data mark, you can score lower. This is because whilst teachers may be able to bring 'star' lessons out of the bag at regular observations; and where planning may look good on paper; and where books can appear marked and up-to-date 'when handed in' – nothing shapes a child's year like the progress they have made. It therefore should be centre stage when a teacher's performance is considered.

We use the word disappointing rather than inadequate. We are not OFSTED and we don't need to use all of their language.

There are lots of proformas that allow you to record your thoughts regarding the teaching you are observing. I offer a simple one for you here. What distinguishes it from some others is the impact box. When you watch a colleague teach you should be judging what progress they have made since the last observation. This is crucial if a dialogue is to be established.

Context	Impact
Have recommendations from last time been successfully implemented?	
Which factors contributed to learning?	
What might you try next time?	
Anything you should consider stopping doing.	

Classroom Support Staff

'Behind every great teacher, there is a great teaching assistant.'
Lorraine Stratton (Teaching Assistant)

I have worked with some that were inspirational and others whom were mundane. What was the difference?

Intelligence and attitude!

And, if you pushed me, I'd choose attitude every time. Every time.

However, a bright teaching assistant who is accommodating, placid and downright amenable is worth their weight in gold.

The single biggest gripe of teaching assistants would appear to be that the school does not invest in their training. We made a point at my school of employing them to 5.15pm on a Monday so they could take part in all after school training along with the teaching staff. It also meant they were present for weekly information briefings.

If you do have talented teaching assistants and they have a degree, I would encourage you beyond measure to get them involved in the Schools Direct route into teaching; and if they don't have a degree, consider sponsoring them to get one. With recruitment an ever growing problem – 'the grow your own' approach is not one to be discounted. Currently, over half of my teaching force started life as a teaching assistant. Often such people are tied to the community in which they live and serve and make excellent loyal colleagues as a consequence.

With ever tightening budgets, some schools have had to choose between having their teaching assistants spending time supporting children in the classroom or alternatively supporting teachers with administrative tasks. They seemingly cannot afford both. Schools are having to be creative. Teaching assistants are having to be flexible, working across classes and year teams. Training is therefore more important than ever. I think if you are faced with hard choices, you will need to ensure particularly that time is well spent whether it be supporting the learner or the teacher (and I think you need a balance of both), so whatever sum you have, you will need to divide it. Not all learners need to be supported; quality first teaching should be adequate. However, I have never met a teacher who did not need to be supported with some clerical tasks, if they are to be deployed in the most effective way, that is.

The worst use of a teaching assistant is the one which sees him or her doing too much for a child, with the child not needing to develop their independence.

I currently have three higher level teaching assistants (HLTAs). None want to progress into teaching, more's the pity. But that is a choice they have made. Avoid using HLTAs (who would be prepared to train) as cheap teachers. Just because you can, does not mean you should.

Whatever your support staff, they will want to be informed of what is going on – and consulted! Ignore them at your peril – they all seek ownership. Let them think they run the school with your blessing – you could do far worse!

Important People (whom you will need on side)

The Business Manager

When I first became a head teacher, I was told the most important relationship in the school to cultivate was that with the caretaker. I think we have moved on. The most significant other for me is the **business manager. They will usually manage your budget, your administrative team and your school's delivery of health and safety.** You need to keep them closer than even the deputy – their sphere of influence is generally wider. How do you do that?

- pay them well
- start each day with them
- remember their birthday
- make them a member of SLT
- use them as a confidante
- give them a team to manage
- tell them things first
- big them up in front of the staff
- be prepared to defer to them when appropriate.

The Local Authority Inspector as the School Improvement Partner

No longer statutory, unless you are in a category, some local authorities persevere with this model.

- Many I have worked with have never been heads themselves. They will often see themselves as pseudo OFSTED. They are not. Don't let them be. They are used in some authorities to challenge and support, which they should do in equal measure. If they are not doing the latter, what do they bring to the table? We have OFSTED to be OFSTED. They should have good local knowledge and therefore be able to point you in the direction of schools that have found solutions to the problems that you face.
- You will need to keep them on side, even if they are in the background. You never know when the tide will turn against you and you will **need them** then.
- As we go to print, the role of the local authority in school improvement is disappearing and private consultants are becoming more widespread. This gives maintained schools the flexibility to choose with whom they will be working and it is, in my view, to be welcomed.

The Chief Executive (CEO) of a MAT

More important than the Local Authority representative, the CEO will be someone to whom you are now directly accountable. This role is evolving and its direct impact upon you will be tempered by how many schools exist in your trust. If there are a hundred schools, you are more likely to come into regular contact with someone working for your Chief Executive. But make no mistake, the Trust will be able to hire and fire much more easily than a board of governors in a maintained school. Ensure they understand your context: this will be invaluable should your pupils' attainment be lower than that of other schools in the trust or dip in one year.

The Deputy

I have had six. I think it is helpful if you like one another. I have known the relationship sour for a range of reasons – some of them unprintable. A breakdown in this relationship is to be avoided for staff will inevitably be tempted to take sides. Deputies have a lot to prove – in my experience they feel people are always judging them, watching them – to see if they are ready for the top job. Undermine a deputy at your peril.

The Caretaker/ Site Manager

The caretaker or site manager nevertheless remains an important relationship. Caretakers are interesting people. If you find yourself with a gem, take care of them:
- don't let staff keep them waiting to lock up the building
- be prepared to chat with them
- remember their birthday and Christmas

In my experience, you are, however, far more likely to have a misery on your hands: some caretakers like to complain – they see it as going with the territory. Indeed, I once had one tell me that it was part of the job to be miserable. Be prepared to stand your ground – if you give an inch, they will take a mile.

Fellow Head Teachers

A trusted network of colleagues will be invaluable. You will quickly come to realise that the challenges you face are shared by other colleagues, including those who work in different contexts. This will make you instantly feel better. In addition, you will be able to learn from what others have tried in different scenarios. A problem shared is very much a problem halved.

Staff Well-being

Before any consideration of sickness and its impact upon the work place, comes a genuine concern for the well-being of one's staff. Absence rates are highest when staff are unhappy at work.

When you have been in post over a year, a brave Head will invite someone into the school to interview his or her staff. The interviews will have at their base, staff well-being.

I offer a selection of questions that might be asked.

- What is your role in this school?

- Which teams are you a part of?

- Do your teams work well together? How might they work better together?

- What happens when something goes wrong in this school?

- Do all staff consistently apply policies?

- Is this a happy place to work? What makes it so?

- Is communication effective in this school?

- Are you clear upon the direction of the school? Can you describe it, naming the key objectives for the year?

- Do you know what your training needs are? Those of your team?

- Are your training needs well met in this school?

- Are whole school INSETs effective? Do they enable you to do a better job?

- (To leaders only.) Are there blockers in this school? Do you know who they are? Do they know who they are?

- What would you change about this school?

- What do you value most about this school?

- (To leaders only.) What do you think is the difference between leadership and management?

- Do leaders in this school lead and manage well?

Following on from this bout of introspection, a report can be assembled and the courageous Head – the confident one – will share the findings with staff. Flying by the seat of your pants time!

Sickness

If you do have a member of staff who has an illness that proves a concern, you will usually have a rate of absence 'trigger point', agreed with the local authority. A referral to Occupational Health is usually the first point of call if the concerns are grounded. In all such discussions with an employee in that position, you will want to walk a fine line between being sympathetic to their predicament and being firm. If the illness is genuine, you will want to be supportive. However, if you have a member of staff who does not come into work as a result of minor ill health that someone else would work through, you will need to set out your expectations moving forward in the clearest terms. Not to, would be doing them, and you, a disservice. However, the thing to remember at all times is to stick with the policy, follow the process. Never have informal or off the record conversations that can come back to bite you. You may find the employee with a troubling sickness record frustrating, annoying even – but you must never show it.

Recruitment

We are facing a recruitment crisis in teaching terms and – with the projected growth in school numbers – it is one that can seemingly only get worse in the decade to come. In my own school, we have looked to train our own through the Direct Access route into teaching. On occasions, this has meant not having these trainees as supernumerary (ie, paired with an existing class teacher but taking the class alone) – we simply couldn't afford to double up. In addition, we have taken HLTAs and employed them as unqualified teachers when we have been unable to recruit qualified staff. This has been the right thing for my school in its current context – an opportunity to grow our own, schooling them in our ways. This has meant some difficult conversations with parents who expect their children to be taught by qualified teachers at each step of their journey through a primary school. But by having those conversations in an honest and positive manner, it is possible to overcome early resistance. It is ironic that the private sector has been able to employ unqualified teachers for as long as any of us can remember.

Grievance/ Disciplinary

Be clear that these are two sides of the same coin. It is often a case of who gets in first. You cannot start a grievance if a disciplinary is under way and vice-versa. There are two kinds of disciplinary when it comes to teachers: capability and conduct. Capability is generally the harder to work through but conduct can be particularly ugly. In a sense, if you find yourself with either a grievance against you or a disciplinary that you are undertaking, you have already lost. You might like to ask yourself how you found yourself in this position. Perhaps you have been unlucky, but it is more often the case that you have made some mistakes along the way. Know what they are so you do not make them again.

Handling a Disciplinary

Whatever the cause, you now find yourself in an enviable position. This is going to be tricky. Not least because you are likely to see the worst in people emerge but in addition, you will come into contact with the union official. Union officials are invariably good at what they do. They are usually well trained and have a liking for confrontation. It always worries me when a head teacher colleague says they like confrontation. Ideally, you should not. It should be an uncomfortable sensation if you are emotionally intelligent. What is there to like? You are putting your authority on the line. It is okay to find that stressful. I have never looked forward to discussions with union representatives. Such occasions are usually the union official's meat and drink; they will be old hands at it, whereas for you it will (hopefully) be a rare occurrence.

So, stop.

Rethink.

Is following a formal route the only way forward? It is not too late.

Can it be avoided?

If not, proceed with caution. You will need to be well prepared and ably supported by a representative from your authority's HR department. Your best friend will be a diary. This will be the diary you have kept since you began to have concerns about a colleague's capability or conduct. It will have nothing else in it. It will be just for that purpose.

There are three things to remember: process, process and process. You must follow it. Make sure you know it, or that you know someone who does.

Responding to a Grievance

Grievances are rare. People avoid them, sometimes even when they should not. I think the main thing to do – which won't be easy at the time – is to imagine the courage that the one with the grievance must have had to muster in order to get to this stage. If you think you have been maligned, say so. But be prepared to be conciliatory where you can. You are going to have to work with this person tomorrow. If you have made mistakes, admit them. They will think more of you if you do.

Section 6: Teaching and Learning

Teaching and Learning

'I said I'd taught him; I didn't say he'd learnt.'

Jaded Y6 teacher

Outstanding Teaching

Outstanding schools have outstanding teaching. Period.

OFSTED says that it has no preferred model for outstanding teaching. I think that's a little disingenuous because they do state what they don't want; so, by implication we can join the dots.

They don't want too much teacher talk.

They don't want low expectations.

Remember, you won't be judged outstanding unless teaching in your school is thought to be outstanding.

What does that look like? It might be better to say what does it feel like? Because there is a feel to it, a buzz. Expectations will certainly be high. Most lessons that fall short of the mark feature a teacher talking at the outset for upwards of 20 minutes (I've seen longer!). There instead needs to be an appropriate balance of talk (teacher and pupil) and children 'doing things' – I call it 'teacher and children talk' – pupils do; teacher talks; pupils do; teacher talks; pupils do – you get the idea! I think the talk should last no longer than the child's age plus one minute. There will be appropriate differentiation and questions will be designed to make children think. Additional adults will be well used: they will have an impact on learning. The children will be making excellent progress. Will there be a wow factor? Yes, I think there will. But that is not to be confused with the teacher acting a part, taking to the centre of the stage – performing. Instead the wow should be focused on the children – are they desperate to learn, is there a thirst for learning that the teacher has created? You will be able to tell from their reactions. Do they say 'yessssss', when told what they are going to be doing? I have recently seen children punch the air when they got something right that had really challenged them. Great to see.

But teaching is no longer just about the lesson. Judgements will increasingly depend upon what inspectors see in books.

Is there breadth and balance to what they are asked to do? Is the work well presented? Are the children asked to develop ideas, do corrections, answer additional questions – and do the teachers respond to what the children then do; and do the children then respond to what the teachers then say – in other words is there a dialogue going on? Conversations, if you like, between pupil and teacher. That is when teaching is outstanding. In our school, we introduced a simple idea of putting a bubble at the end of children's work. The teacher would write in the bubble, asking the child do to something; and the child, in turn, would respond in a bubble. For example:

The quality of the bubbles is important. There is no point in just giving 'MOTS' – more of the same. If a child has got 17 calculations out of 20 correct, what will be achieved by giving them three more to do? It is far better to extend their thinking or maybe even get them to first encounter a new idea that will feature in the next lesson.

And what pupils say to inspectors about learning and teaching has significant impact on judgements made.

How do teachers help you to learn?

What gets in the way of your learning?

What would you change about your lessons if you could?

Is homework worthwhile?

Learning

Much has been written on learning elsewhere following painstaking research. I just want to reiterate a few key points.

 So much of what we do in the classroom needs to be 'revisited' as a matter of routine if children are not to forget what they have been taught. We liken this to the act of a circus performer who attempts to spin a succession of plates at the same time. As he makes his way along a line adding a new spinning plate to a pole, he needs to run back to give the earlier plates spun a little touch with his finger; if he doesn't, they will lose momentum, stop spinning and crash to the ground. Too often, we see children in schools whose plates have stopped spinning. Too many teachers march on and do not pay enough attention to ensuring what has already been learned is not forgotten.

Learning styles

There is a huge amount of information available on learning styles, much of it contradictory. Some, such as Will Ryan in his book, Leadership with a Purpose, argue that learners can be divided into three preferred learning styles:

Visually orientated learners respond well to	Auditory orientated learners respond well to	Kinaesthetically orientated learning respond well to
The written word Diagrams Pictures Videos Wall charts and posters	The spoken word Lectures Audio tapes Discussion Sound effects	Movement Hands on activities Designing and creative activities Role-play and drama

Building on this, some people have jumped to the conclusion that if a pupil shows a preference for say, auditory learning, then everything should be presented to them in that way, leading to a fad for planning for the different learning styles in every lesson. In my view this was taking things too far.

Others, such as Cedar Riener and Daniel Willingham, argue that there is no neuropsychological evidence for learning styles and, specifically, for tailoring instruction to suit each pupil's preferred style.

Some children I have taught do indeed appear to have had a leaning towards one style rather than another. Speaking personally, I prefer visual and audio tasks. I detest practical tasks and put myself at the back of any group activity that features such a kinaesthetic approach.

My view is that some things are better learned in a particular way. For example, the Bayeux Tapestry is a fantastic original source for learning about Normans. However, although there are illustrations on the Tapestry of soldiers wearing chain mail, having a real piece of chain mail that children can feel the weight of in their hands is a much better way of helping them to understand what is was like to be dressed as a Norman soldier, whether they are a kinaesthetic learner or not.

Whether you subscribe to the learning styles theory or not, providing a variety of learning experiences, as shown in the table above, makes lessons more interesting and engaging. Too often I see teachers talking 'at' children for half the lesson, using visual stimuli for less than 10% of the lesson and where the only 'doing' ever is writing. We need to see more variety in our classrooms.

Only this way will we grow each child's talents, which can best be described as inherent in Gardner's nine intelligences, again to be found in Ryan's book.

Verbal Linguistic Facility for word and language in speaking, reading and writing.	**Logical Mathematical** Capacity for inductive or deductive thinking, use of numbers.	**Visual Spatial** Ability to visualise objects and spatial dimensions and create internal images.
Bodily Kinaesthetic High control over physical motion, adept with hands, enjoys active involvement.	**Musical Rhythmic** Ability to recognise tonal patterns, sensitive to rhythm and beat.	**Interpersonal** Strong social skills and relationship, a sensitive listener.
Intrapersonal Ability to be reflective and intuitive, self-knowledge and reflection	**Naturalistic** Enjoys outdoors, conducts own enquiries, links learning to natural world.	**Existential** Sensitivity, seeks answers to deep questions relating to human existence.

Bloom's Taxonomy

No consideration of how children learn would be complete without a reference to Bloom's Taxonomy. This seminal piece of work can usefully guide so much of what we do, although, I estimate that fewer than 5% of primary teachers regularly refer to it. Often overworked, they presumably leave it to published schemes to do it for them. But how we question children – and the taxonomy describes it so well – is crucial to the interactions that go on in our classrooms. Were we to examine the types of questions posed by many of our teachers, I think we would find most were pitched at the lower end of Bloom's scale – the recall and understanding. I have reproduced Bloom's taxonomy chart for you below, just in case you yourself have become unfamiliar with it:

Combining parts to make a new whole	Create
Judging the value of information or ideas	Evaluate
Breaking down information into component parts	Analyse
Applying the facts, rules, concepts and ideas	Apply
Understanding what the facts mean	Understand
Recognising and recalling facts	Remember

Outstanding schools keep Bloom's Taxonomy uppermost in their mind.

Lesson Planning

The importance of effective planning cannot be overstated. And don't buy into those voices that will have you believe that you are constraining learning by having a detailed plan. It is not a straight-jacket and, as we always say, you can't come away from a plan unless you have one. There are all sorts of planning tools and templates on the market. My advice, design your own! Think of something that displays your priorities and allows you to move forward together as a staff.

I include overleaf an example of a plan that was designed by my staff and which saw an outstanding lesson emerge; in part, as a result of their thorough planning.

Planning needs to be as thorough as teachers can make it! Don't expect the same level of detail in non-core subjects. It is not sustainable. But the uncomfortable truth – in these days of workload and pressure – is that outstanding planning is the cornerstone of outstanding lessons. Cut other things from teacher's duties to give them maximum time for planning and marking. Together with delivery, this is what their job should be about: cut the record keeping that can be cut, but insist upon detailed planning and marking.

Example of Planning that Led to Outstanding Lesson for OFSTED

ST.BEDE'S PRIMARY SCHOOL

Subject: Maths
Term: Spring 1st half
Set: Mrs Roberts and Mrs Dayson
Lesson: Combination locks – solving mathematical problems (5th February 2015)

Learning Objectives (LO):	Resources:
● I can use a systematic and logical approach to solve problems (main activity)	● Laptops, whiteboards and pens
	● A4 Squared Paper
Success Criteria (SC):	● Broken Calculator Problem
For the main activity I (the children) have:	● Broken Calculator Problems A and B (for extension and differentiation)
● accurately applied my mathematical knowledge	● Combination Locks Test Problem No.1
● used an efficient and clear method to record my working out	● Combination Locks Test Problem No.2
● broke problems down into manageable steps, including choosing the order in which to solve the problems	● Combination Lock differentiated questions (Mr Smith's, Mrs Brown's and Mr Taylor's Locks)
● been able to explain how I found an answer / solution to a problem	● Extension Lock Problems
Type of differentiation: Supported by **CT** using differentiated questions	
Key Vocabulary: Systematic, Logical, Ordered, Efficient, Method, Clear	**Additional adult focus:**

Begin lesson by introducing the **LO**, **SC** and key words. Use **PW /DT** to allow children to discuss their understanding of the key words. Feedback and clarify the meanings of each key word.

CT to explain in today's lesson children will have to solve a range of problems; use this to introduce the following **KQs/PW/DT** (to be discussed with a partner and then feedback) :
● What do you have to do when solving a problem in maths?
● Is this the same for worded and non-worded problems?

Use feedback to elicit the need for:
● Reading the problem through (more than once if needed) so that you know what is expected
● Understand the problem / Decide upon which operation(s) / number of steps you will need to use
● Choose an appropriate method / operation
● Solve the problem (including estimate)
● Answer the problem
● Check that your answer is reasonable

Use slide 7 and 8 to introduce today's work:

Explain that the three people are upset because each one of them is locked out of something or somewhere. Unfortunately they can't call a locksmith to help them as the locks they need to open are combination locks and they need the children's help. Explain to children that this is a real problem that hundreds of people face each day and today we are going to find the combinations of some different locks.

CT to explain that before the children can actually try to find the codes to some real combination locks, they need to have a go at one or two practice locks to see if they are up to the job. Display the problem 'Combination Locks Test Problem No.1' (slide 9) on the board. Tell children that these are the clues to help us find the code for the first lock.

KQ/PW/DT What is the first thing I / we need to do? (read through the problems /codes) **CT** to read through the problem and get a child re-read the problem:
● The hundred's digit is double the thousand's digit
● The thousand's digit is the number of sides on a semi-circle
● All the digits are even
● The hundred's digit is 50% of the last digit
● The ten's digit is between the ten's and unit's digits

KQ/PW/DT What do I have to do? (to find each of the digits that make up the code for the lock)

KQ/PW/DT What knowledge or skills will I be using? (doubling, halving, knowledge of shape, percentages and properties of numbers)

KQ/PW/DT Thinking back to the **LO**, what method will I be using? (clear, systematic and logical)

KQ/PW/DT Can I estimate my answer? (elicit that it isn't always possible to estimate and many of today's problems will not be able to be estimated)

CT to model how to solve the problem, 'Combination Locks Test Problem No.1', using a systematic method. Use non-interactive whiteboard to show method.

On completion of modelling make clear what it is that made your method systematic.

If children are not secure after **CT** modelling, use the second test problem on slide 10. However, this problem should be worked through with greater pupil input.

Introduce Independent Work:

Children to work in ability pairs using a systematic and logical method to solve the differentiated problems set out below. Use A3 squared paper to record workings / methods (these must be clear). Make children aware that they may have to feedback their methods used to solve some of today's problems.
• 	Mrs Brown's locks (**LA** and **MA**) These children can have their maths dictionaries open in Fronter can self-differentiate / access to definitions of mathematical terms (eg squared numbers)
• 	Mr Taylor's locks (**HA** and **G&T**)

CT to initially work with the **MA** group but once happy they are secure in their understanding **CT** to move round table groups to ascertain children's level of understanding and to check children are recording their methods systematically.

Simplification:	Extension: G&T children to solve the extension combination locks problems.

Plenary:

Ask some **KQ**s:

What prior knowledge did you use in today's lesson?

If you look at another pair's squared paper what would you expect to see?

Ask children to swap work (with another pair): have they set out their work clearly? How do you know?

Do you think they have a good understanding of today's work? How do you know?

Children to share some of their methods used to solve some of the problems.

Ask: Can anyone show me their method for solving the problem?

Children to act as critical friends. **KQ**s: Is their method clear? Have they been systematic?

Children to use partner talk to evaluate what they have done in today's lesson. Use the **KQ**s below to prompt children's discussion:

What skills have you been applying /using?

What have you learnt?

What did you find difficult?

What tips would you give to someone answering these types of word problems?

Feedback

End session by:

1) Focusing on Next Steps: Ask **KQ** to encourage the children to think of any targets or things they would do differently if they did this sort of activity again?

2) Ask children to evaluate today's lesson using the forum in the **MLE**; remind children they should try to respond to the prompt in the forum.

Key

KQ	Key Question	**MLE**	Managed Learning Environment
CT	Class Teacher	**LA**	Lower Ability
PW	Paired Work	**MA**	Middle Ability
DT	Differentiated Task	**HA**	Higher Ability
LO	Learning Objective		
SC	Success Criteria		

Head teacher: The clue is in the word

As a head teacher, you will want to be teaching. For all sorts of reasons:
- it demonstrates to the staff that you are one of them (you understand the pressures they face and the many demands that are made of them);
- it shows you are accountable;
- it signifies to parents that you are in touch;
- it enables children to interact with you on a more relaxed level.

There are seemingly five types of teaching that head teachers engage in:
- the head teacher covering for illness;
- the one-off release lesson, as a good will gesture;
- PPA cover, usually once or twice a week;
- modelling lessons;
- the head teacher who takes a maths or English class each day throughout the year.

Of the five, the last two are arguably the ones that will bring the most dividends. Modelling lessons is really putting yourself on the line – very few colleagues do it. If you pull it off successfully, you will earn great respect. Your ability to do so will depend in large part upon how fresh you keep your skills set. The best way to stay sharp is to follow the fifth route – teach maths or English every day to the same group of children each year – thus assuming responsibility for their learning over time. Yes, it will be a significant chunk of your day, but it will be time very well spent. If you aren't deskilled, you can speak with more authority in staff discussions.

'Who said I'd lost it!'

Pupil Behaviour

You are going to need your pupils to display excellent behaviour in school if your teaching and learning strategies are to hit home.

I offer the following:

Have one clear set of warnings and sanctions uniformly followed across the school.	Do not deviate from this unless you are dealing with disability.
Use praise to highlight to the class those children who are doing the right thing.	'I liked it when you ...' 'Can we all see how x is working well ...' ' 'Great hands-up from ...' Use the school's reward system.
Set your expectations high and articulate them clearly from the outset of the lesson.	Be positive rather than negative. List the behaviours you do want to see rather than those you don't.
Don't seek to justify your decisions to children – never negotiate with children.	There is no need. You are the person in authority.
Choose the right things to check with the use of sanctions – look in the behaviour log (there needs to be one) to see when other teachers use it;	We don't put children in a behaviour log for swinging on a chair. Staff should use any such log sparingly but well.
Be persistently persistent.	You have to stay on top of things. It is hard work but it is always worth going the extra mile.
Raise your voice sparingly.	If you over use your voice, it loses effect over time.
Be well prepared.	Good behaviour management is rooted in good preparation.
Have high expectations.	'Act' surprised when children do something inappropriate – you can then work your way up to disappointment. It is a useful first step.
Be a presence in the classroom.	Never talk over children, wait for silence. Count 3, 2, 1 or raise your hand with the children following suit. Insist upon it.
Choose your battles carefully.	If you sanction every piece of low level disappointing behaviour, you will quickly become overwhelmed and end up with unmanageable number of pupils on amber; this will in itself undermine you. Tactically ignore at the right times. This is a tricky one. At first it sounds like a contradiction to being consistent, but it is not. It comes with experience.
Reward those children whose behaviour is consistently good.	The ubiquitous traffic light system is very effective if used in every single classroom. But introduce a green 'plus', where the names of children whose behaviour is outstanding can be placed. Follow it up with a sticker or certificate. Have a clear sanction for those children who work their way to red.

How To Organise Pupils

If your school is big enough, I would advocate setting for maths and reading, not writing.

- Maths because children need to go at different paces. Yes, in an ideal world there would be a minimum entitlement where the bar is set high – the bottom set pupils will need to be doing much of what the tops are doing, but they will necessarily need to move forward at a different pace.
- Reading because they should be accessing texts that are pitched at their level, not the level below or above.

Writing should always be mixed ability. Pupils need to be exposed to the rich ideas and vocabulary of more able children if they are to grow and develop. I know that research suggest that only more able children benefit from ability groupings or setting but that is not my experience.

Boys versus girls? We have organised our pupils by gender and seen very positive results. Boys learn differently to girls – they typically like drama featuring role play, action novels and a particularly competitive atmosphere. Worth a try!

With the latest OFSTED dashboards, the focus upon groups' attainment and progress has become sharper still. Some pupils used to be what I called 'golden ticket' children: convert their prior attainment scores into value added and you were more likely than less to be judged a success. With the new dashboards, every child would appear to be a golden ticket child. However, even then, there are some children who are more 'golden' than others. Disadvantaged children are of crucial importance – as are, to a lesser extent, SEN support pupils. And the argument is simple – double the resources (Pupil Premium and High Needs Funding), then double the progress that is expected. Do your teachers know who the disadvantaged children or SEN plus children are?

'At last, we can get on with some work without the usual silly noises!'

Inclusion

'I never felt my son was really included. He spent lots of his time away from the class and other children began to see him as different.'

Parent of Child with Special Educational Needs

I found myself chatting to a fellow head teacher over coffee at a local authority conference. I can't remember how we got on to the conversation but SATs results and positions in league tables came up. Unlike me, she worked in a school in the leafy suburbs. Working in deepest, darkest council estate land, I was no threat to her. She was, she told me, vying to be first again this year, having slipped to second the previous September. But, she said to me, in a manner that was quite matter of fact, I know I can trump the school who beat me last year because they have a child with Down's Syndrome in this year's cohort. Did she smile, sensing victory? It made me feel uncomfortable. Dealing with the least able in society – those who face the biggest challenges: outstanding primary schools are meant to do just that! Putting briefly aside no less demanding but more visible physical disabilities, it is a fact that 1 in 10 children aged 2–15 have a mental health issue with which they are dealing; and 1 in 7 adults has a personality disorder. Do we look to include such people in what we do? Because if your school isn't going to do it, then who is?

> **That's something that outstanding schools do: <u>include everyone</u>. Good schools try, but they don't always succeed.**

Let's have a story. It depicts how children themselves regard their peers who have special needs. You want your pupils to see them as individuals in their own right – as somebody with whom they would like to be friends. It's as simple as that.

Davey's Story (an assembly story for children)

Davey had been looking forward to his induction day at St Agatha's although it would be fair to say that he was apprehensive about it too. He had heard stories about the older boys making fun of the younger kids. Davey didn't want to be singled out and embarrassed in front of people.

His mum had said not to worry. He knew other boys who were going, which was true. There was Thomas, Luke and Pete. That morning he showered early and sat down to breakfast with a heavy heart. He had butterflies in his stomach, there was no denying it.

'What is it love?' said Mum, ruffling his hair.

'I'm nervous,' he replied. 'There are going to be so many people I don't know. 'What happens if I don't fit in? I don't want to be on my own, left out.'

'Don't be daft,' said Mum. 'You'll soon make new friends in September, once you have settled in.'

They had to get a coach to the secondary school. He had arranged to meet with the other boys at the bus stop. Mum dropped him 100 metres away; he didn't want to be seen being dropped off. It was time to act like a Y7 kid; he knew that much. Being seen with your Mum didn't fit and Davey wanted to fit in – more than anything else.

When he arrived at the stop, the other three were already there. Pete was chatting up Louise Parsons, who Davey knew but not well. The bus drew up and the driver appeared at the door.

'Right you 'orrible lot' he declared, 'like I said to the others, behave or you're off. Comprende?'

The kids bundled on. Sitting in the first seat was Stephen Tompkins. He was in Davey's class but he was what the other Mums called 'slow'. He hung around with Clive and Damien, who the children knew to have special needs too. But those two boys were going to St Cuthbert's. Stephen was on his own and it showed.

'Shall we sit with Stephen?' Davey turned and mumbled to Luke. Pete overheard.

'You're having a laugh,' he said. 'There are women to impress; we're not sitting with a loser.'

The boys swept past Stephen and Davey hoped the tall boy hadn't heard what had been said about him.

When they got to the school, there were teachers to meet them at the gate and they were marshalled to their taster classes like penguins waddling after one another in a line at the zoo. The first class was history and to Davey's horror there wasn't one person he knew in the class. His nerves returned. His heart was pounding and he felt as self-conscious as a vegetarian at a barbecue. He stared down at the worksheet in front of him. The words seemed to jump about on the page. He hoped the teacher – a tall man with a booming voice – wouldn't choose him to answer a question. He didn't and after 30 minutes of tension Davey was released along with the other kids into the corridor. There were bodies everywhere. At the end of the corridor, Davey spied Stephen on his own. He looked vulnerable and all at once, for the second time that day, Davey felt sorry for the boy. But then Luke appeared, followed by Pete – and Davey lost sight of Stephen.

Davey's day wasn't going well. He hadn't liked the feeling of being in a class full of strangers. And he was starting to worry about Stephen. He didn't like the fact that the boy was on his own. He, Davey, could do something about it but he knew the other lads wouldn't like that. And that was the problem. Davey didn't want to lose the friendship of the other three boys. He needed them. The remainder of his friends from St Mary's were going to other schools. But he felt mean and he didn't like the feeling.

At lunchtime, the children were allowed to eat their lunch wherever as there was no dining hall. The four boys chose a classroom that had a group of girls sitting in it. 'This looks like our spot,' said Pete and proceeded to get his sandwiches out. The boys started eating. Davey couldn't help but wonder where Stephen was. Was he somewhere on his own? Suddenly he walked by in the corridor.

'Quick.' said Luke. 'It's Stephen, duck down.' The boys all did as they were motioned, Davey too. Stephen returned to the classroom door but only seeing the girls, he walked away. The girls who had watched all this began to laugh and Pete, sensing his chance, moved in for the kill. He was soon playing the fool and the girls laughed all the more.

But Davey still felt mean.

In the afternoon, Davey found himself on his own again – this time for music and French. He hated being without friends for the second time in the same day. But the teachers were nice enough and he was praised for the work he produced in his books, which made him feel much better.

At the end of the day, he sat with his friends on the bus back home. They shared their stories of their days. He had survived. He felt relieved.

When he got in, Mum and Dad quizzed him on his day. And without meaning to, he burst into tears. Mum gave him a squeeze, which made him feel worse and immediately gave him hiccups. The stupidity of the situation – him with tears and hiccups – made them all start laughing and at once he felt better.

'Let's break this down into manageable chunks,' said Dad.

'Tell us about something that went well,' said Mum. That was easy. The French teacher said she was pleased with my work, reported Davey.

'See,' said Dad, 'it wasn't all bad.'

'What was the worse bit?' Davey immediately thought about being in lessons on his own. But before he could answer, another thought sprung to mind; it was of Stephen. Davey had treated him badly and he knew it. Davey had had to spend some lessons without friendly faces, Stephen had had to spend his whole day like that, he was guessing.

He told Mum and Dad.

'Why can't you have Stephen as a friend?' Dad asked.

Davey said nothing.

Mum said, 'He's different to the other kids. He's slow. He has trouble speaking and he is gangly. He moves in a funny way,' she added by way of explanation. It was true, Stephen was not a cool kid.

'Not cool eh?' said Dad, reading Davey's mind.

'Don't tell me, you want to look like one of the lads and being with Stephen will affect your street cred.'

'That's about it,' mumbled Davey – just a little ashamed.

'But it didn't make you happy today, did it?' said Dad. 'Something tells me you have a choice to make. If you're friends with Stephen the other lads will either stick with you or they won't. Those that don't aren't worth bothering with.'

All at once Davey knew Dad was right.

Davey had made his mind up. He would meet the lads in the normal way at the bus stop when they returned in September but this time he would be sitting next to Stephen. Davey hoped to make lots of new friends at secondary school and Stephen would be the first.

Every child, like Stephen, on your register could usefully have a pupil passport (see example on page 118–119). This enables teachers to quickly grasp the needs of a child for whom they have just accepted responsibility.

Outstanding primary schools make room for this kind of provision.

Example Pupil Passport

Pupil: Amy Smith D.O.B. 20.3.09	My photo	Pupil Passport	St. Bede's Catholic Primary School & Nursery
Class: 4K		Date passport created: September 2017	Date of update: September 2018
Area(s) of need: Cognition and learning		I would like you to know that: • I can read most of my Phase 3 and Phase 5 phonemes. • I can use my number bonds to solve problems within 20. • I can understand and discuss the stories I read.	I find it difficult: • To remember letter blends at the end of words. • To recall the words I want to write in a sentence. • To recognise all numbers to 100. • To spell high frequency words consistently.

It would help me if you could:	I will help myself by:	My parents/carers will help me by:
Create word banks on my ipad for big writing.	Using my talking tin.	Chopping the sounds I hear at the end of words.
Provide word grids.	Playing memory games on my ipad.	Playing memory games.
Remind me to use my talking tin.	Reading at home.	Reading with me regularly.
Ask me to recall things in order, requiring more and more detail as time goes on.		Helping me to practise spellings and words sent home, using multisensory techniques.
Using the my word mat/word book to help with spelling.		

Outside Agency Support and other details:	Attainment Information:								
	Previous end of year results			My latest results			My end of year targets		
Outside Agency Support		Writing	Maths	Reading	Writing	Maths	Reading	Writing	Maths
• Amy has been assigned an iPad (iPad 8). She should use the iPad when writing whenever possible. There are also apps on the iPad for cognition and memory skills. The iPad should be written into Amy's SEN Support plan. • Amy has been seen by the EP (11.9.14) • Amy is seen by the school's assigned SALT • Amy should use her Talking Tin when composing sentences.	4C	4C	4C	4C	4C	4B	4B	4B	4B

Curriculum

I can remember when I first started teaching, cross-curricular topics were all the rage. Teachers would think of a theme – Transport, Trees, Space – and try to link the work they would set the children to the theme. They often produced a topic web that would show all the history, geography, maths, etc that would be covered. It didn't matter often if that was the maths or English that the children then needed; the question was, did it fit with the theme?

The teachers' intentions were good: they were trying to give the children contextualised learning. Such learning helps children to better understand what they are being taught and can, quite simply, be more fun for the children. There is a lot to be said for enjoyment in the classroom. Memory, as Alan Peat continually tells us, is associative: we remember things best when we can associate those things with something that will stick with us. For example, enjoying doing something is great for associate memory. However, the links between the areas were often tenuous and there were few activities that actually simultaneously taught objectives from different subjects at an appropriate pitch and level. HMI, of course, discovered a lack of continuity and progression in the teaching of many subjects at this time through this topic approach and so the National Curriculum was borne. Most, though not all, schools then opted for a subject specific approach and planned and delivered within the constraints of a subject based time table. Some schools have continued with this straight jacket approach. It is a shame because work that truly features cross curricular dimensions – an intertwining, if you like of curricular objectives and as a consequence a merging of content can be innovative and exciting. I enjoyed using 1881 Census returns to teach the children about Victorians and in order to come to draw conclusions about family size, I had to teach the children about finding 'ranges and averages' and representing information in graphs and tables – all of which was identified on the maths programme of study for the age and ability of children whom I was teaching.

With the Excellence and Enjoyment materials that were produced, there was a sense that cross-curricular content could re-emerge with 'official blessing' and that OFSTED would respond positively to it. I'm not sure it really caught on and the Excellence and Enjoyment movement is long since forgotten.

Cross curricular work, with subject progression rigour at its heart, is hard to plan and deliver well; it is easy to do it badly. How do you ensure that the links you make between subjects are worthwhile and are rooted in the programmes of study that you are required to teach to children of that age? Some schools have used the International Primary Curriculum to deliver an integrated approach, whereas others have designed their own topic based studies. The following integrated curriculum map for parents comes from a school where I am a governor. It is inviting and less dry for children (and teachers!) than a discrete unconnected subject discipline approach.

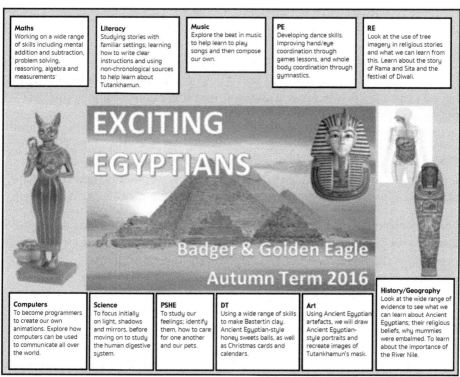

Maths
Working on a wide range of skills including mental addition and subtraction, problem solving, reasoning, algebra and measurements.

Literacy
Studying stories with familiar settings; learning how to write clear instructions and using non-chronological sources to help learn about Tutankhamun.

Music
Explore the beat in music to help learn to play songs and then compose our own.

PE
Developing dance skills. Improving hand/eye coordination through games lessons, and whole body coordination through gymnastics.

RE
Look at the use of tree imagery in religious stories and what we can learn from this. Learn about the story of Rama and Sita and the festival of Diwali.

EXCITING EGYPTIANS

Badger & Golden Eagle
Autumn Term 2016

Computers
To become programmers to create our own animations. Explore how computers can be used to communicate all over the world.

Science
To focus initially on light, shadows and mirrors, before moving on to study the human digestive system.

PSHE
To study our feelings; identify them, how to care for one another and our pets.

DT
Using a wide range of skills to make Bastertin clay. Ancient Egyptian-style honey sweets balls, as well as Christmas cards and calendars.

Art
Using Ancient Egyptian artefacts, we will draw Ancient Egyptian-style portraits and recreate images of Tutankhamun's mask.

History/Geography
Look at the wide range of evidence to see what we can learn about Ancient Egyptians; their religious beliefs, why mummies were embalmed. To learn about the importance of the River Nile.

Taken from St. Mary's Academy, Shenfield

Even the above example has some shortfalls with some subject provision being stand alone. It comes from an outstanding school but even they found it difficult to integrate each area purposefully.

I think the commercial publishers have missed a trick here; they could have commissioned such cross-curricular materials but many chose rather to stick to subject disciplines often isolated from one another. The use of a set fiction text to inspire learning in other curriculum disciplines can, I think, be particularly enjoyable for children. In recent years, my own school has invested in sets of fiction titles – real books – for the whole class to read and enjoy and a lot of work in other subjects has usefully been generated with appropriate rigour and children have made accelerated progress as a result – their imagination and thirst for learning having been ignited.

I like the idea of a stunning starter, marvellous middle and fabulous finish that lots of schools are now using to structure the curriculum focus the children will undertake. Again, it is inviting!

How to ensure a balanced curriculum that has breadth is a perennial problem. Schools that face huge pressure to raise or maintain standards in English or maths, can understandably squeeze the curriculum, particularly in Y6. In my experience, it is history and geography that have taken the hardest cuts. Whilst I understand the pressures that schools are under, this is a great pity. Some schools have sought to integrate history and geography into English lessons – in particular writing lessons; whilst this can serve a purpose, I think you always do well to ask yourself is what I am teaching history or geography, or is it English? The problem is compounded because there is a dearth of good resources for history and geography with the major publishers largely ignoring the market since the late 1990s. Schools have had to be creative and some have been more successful than others.

PSHE is inserted into some other subjects in some schools but treated as a standalone subject in others. Either approach can work but it is important that your leader for this area can show where and how the subject is being delivered.

The term mastery is currently being used to describe different things by schools. If we are not careful we will be into 'The Emperor's New Clothes' territory where everyone is talking about it but can't actually see it. Some say mastery when what they mean is mastery with greater depth – ie, the work of what we used to call the more able child. Rather, mastery is the threshold that we expect the vast majority of children to attain and mastery is about securing this in a unit of work before we move on. There have to be some limitations of course or we might never move on. Maybe we should be aiming for 80% of children being secure or all children 80% secure (different things) before tackling new material. This would be a step forward from the spend three weeks on this and two weeks on that rigid model that saw some children forging ahead in their understanding whilst others, too many, remained behind. The government would seemingly have us believe that all children should be capable of attaining this mastery level or are they bluffing? I do not subscribe to this view. Whilst other education systems may have a shorter 'tail' of lower attainment than we, I have worked with some children who would not be able to 'master' the curriculum – the standards set within it – whatever the quality of teaching and interventions made on their behalf. Such children are below average. To try and pretend this isn't so is to put untenable pressure on teachers. The real battles lie with children who are 'underachieving', not those who are just working at their level, which happens to be lower than that of their peers.

Outstanding schools have a thematic approach to curriculum delivery.

The Learning Walk

Learning Walks have become the latest thing. Everyone is doing them. However, it is worth bearing in mind that you will be bombarded with images when undertaking one. They are useful. They give you a snapshot overview of what is going on. You won't be able to tackle all the shortcomings you see or celebrate all of the successes. Such walks are often a case of 'sensory overload', as one colleague called it. You will need to focus and have a theme; it should complement your school improvement plan: pupil engagement, the learning environment, the child with SEN, the role of the learning assistant or the pace of the lesson. You will think of others. Let colleagues know the focus. You will want to reduce their stress. Learning Walks should not be about trying to catch people out: a good staff won't need to be kept on their toes and you will have a good staff, won't you? You will want colleagues to have the opportunity to shine. Don't overdo the walks – once a term, no more – ideally in the half-term you are not observing them teach a particular lesson. Share the strengths observed with the whole team at a staff briefing shortly after the walk(s) and pick up on areas for common development.

Some Dos and Don'ts:

Do smile.

Do talk to the children, whatever the focus.

Don't spend more than fifteen minutes in any one classroom.

Do talk to all the adults in the room.

Don't take a clip board! In fact, don't write at all. You are not inspecting.

Do make mental notes – write it down as soon as you are out of the room; if you can't remember it, don't stay so long!

Do comment upon the positives that you see there and then.

Don't say anything that could be construed as negative – there will be a time and a place.

Do give feedback to all staff as soon as possible without identifying people by name.

Do ask subtle questions if you don't understand something.

'D' is for Data!

Nothing gets an OFSTED inspector more excited than data.

Outstanding schools know their data and use it to propel better performance.

It's difficult to know, at the time of writing, exactly where we will be going with data analysis post levels, unless you have already decided upon a system to take its place. If you have, you might want to consider whether you can ascribe points to your new criteria. Points make prizes, as they used to say: or, in the more modern context of education, we are used to calculating average point scores to show progress. In our school we have assigned points to our new levels for reading, mathematics and writing. The table below shows how:

Points awarded to each sub-level

1c	1b	1a
11	12	13
2c	2b	2a
14	15	16
3c	3b	3a
17	18	19
4c	4b	4a
20	21	22
5c	5b	5a
23	24	25
6c	6b	6a
26	27	28

Using these point scores we can work out a mean average for each class each term by taking the point score of each pupil and we can then calculate how many points progress has been made by the class since last term. We then produce something we 'daringly' call flight plans and cockpits for each class and teacher based on their class' points scores. Our OFSTED (February 2015) described the idea as 'innovative' – a special word, as we have previously discussed.

See pages 127–8 for a sample Reading Flight Plan and Cockpit.

I am not advocating that you adopt the idea yourself. What matters is that you think of something original for your school that will summarise progress made in each year group and by groups within that group. If you just use what has been commercially published, the inspectors won't see anything innovative in what you are doing. You must show this in a life that is post levels. You must be inventive: designing something that is summative in terms of data. How else will you measure progress?

Governors and teachers find the flight plan and cockpit summaries useful and they are a good starting point for discussions by colleagues at termly reviews of children's progress.

A key to judgements
We measure attainment, which we call 'altitude' (see table on page 124). We calculate a mean average each term by totalling all the individual scores gained by pupils and dividing by the number of pupils in the class.

We measure progress, which we call 'speed' by subtracting from the mean point score for a class the mean point score from the preceding term.

We use the following table for judging speed (progress).

	Thresholds	Speed
Mean Point Score Gain Since Last Term	>3.1	Accelerated
Mean Point Score Gain Since Last Term	2.8-3.1	Smooth
Mean Point Score Gain Since Last Term	< 2.8	Slow

The Head teacher as the Champion of Standards

Although you may not control the mechanics – others can do that (though I prefer to do it myself) – you must be the one who has a keen eye on the progress of each individual child. You should know what they are expected to achieve at each point of their development. In this way you can tell if they are on track to achieve what should be expected of them – given their entry point and displayed potential along the way. I write to parents and meet with them each January if their child's progress is not on track. I invite the maths and English subject leaders to join me. The meetings take place during the day and so I release colleagues to be with me. I even write letters to employers, if necessary, asking them to release parents to meet. These meetings don't replace the parent/ teacher consultations that will be routine in your school. I am not trying to supplant the role of the teacher, rather to complement it. Good teachers will not feel threatened when they see your sincerity. It sends a powerful message out to parents as to who is looking out for their child – in part, you are! Never lose sight of this objective – along with finance and health and safety, it should be your number one priority.

Middle Set Y5 Reading Flight Plan 2016/7 Miss Davies

SUMMER

	PP	SEN	AOE	Y2	Y4	Autumn	Autumn	Spring	Spring	Summer	Summer
Children who should reach a 5b											
Tommy Jones			TFA	2b	4b	58	5b	55	5b	70	5b
Diane Fulman			TFA	2b	4b	53	5b	49	5b	64	5b
Charity Smith			TFA	2b	4b	60	5b	44	5b	67	5b
Andrew Baker			TFA	2b	4b	62	5b	55	5b	83	5a
Cheryl Thompson			BTFA	2b	4b	60	5b	52	5b	90	5a
Dwane Edwards			TFA	2b	4b	46	5b	37	5b	69	5b
Susie Peters			TFA	2b	4b	45	5b	47	5b	66	5b
Tessa Jones	x		TFA	2b	4b	46	5b	53	5b	68	5b
Peter Perkins			BTFA	2b	4b	43	5b	34	5b	66	5b
Brendon Rodgers		x	TFA	2b	4b	59	5b	53	5b	75	5a
Michele Munday	x		TFA	2b	4b	57	5b	54	5b	81	5a
David Roshier			TFA	2b	4b	66	5b	55	5b	79	5a
Children who are aiming for 5b with tutoring support Thursdays (9)											
Anne Palmer			BTFA	2c	4c	28	5b	35	5b	56	5b
Jenny Bedford			BTFA	2c	4c		5c	30	5b	49	5b
Edward Simpkins			BTFA	2b	4c	53	5b	54	5b	72	5b
Toby Baker	x		TFA	2b	4c	36	5b	41	5b	55	5b
Janet Rolls			BTFA	2b	4c	43	5b	41	5b	52	5b
Harry Davids			TFA	2b	4c	49	5b	43	5b	49	5b
Ryan Long			BTFA	1	4c	39	5b	43	5b	70	5b
Andrew Wyatt		x	BTFA	2c	4c	43	5b	37	5b	46	5b
Lee Grover			BTFA	2c	4c	46	5b	44	5b	68	5b
21					20.57			24.0		4	24.25
								3.43			3.68

**Destination:
Where are we heading?**

**Fuel:
What input are we giving?**
Every child a reader
Extra teacher
Saturday school

Trajectory
Climbing
2.68

**Speed:
Progress**
27.00

**Altitude:
Attainment**

SATS

All schools are different. They operate under different pressures. But there is one constant: the further you are up the league table, the safer management feel. SATs matter, big time.

Context is everything. Schools in leafy suburbs can afford to make all the right noises about a broad and balanced curriculum. They can ensure that history and geography for example – which tend to be the poor relation in the modern primary curriculum – are featured properly in the timetable. As a head teacher who has mostly no challenging circumstances in which to work, I prefer to lengthen the school day rather than squeeze foundation subjects. In all of the schools I have run, I have paid school staff generously – and you need to be generous – to stay behind on two evenings each week in order to teach an additional hour's English or maths to those children who need an extra boost. I call such sessions 'tutoring' – a label that will appeal to aspirational parents – and offer them free of charge. I am clear with parents that, without the extra support, their child is unlikely to be ready for the next step in their education. I have only ever known a 95% or higher take up rate. Lately, I have introduced both Saturday schools and Easter schools to serve the same purpose – a targeted boost.

At the time of writing, the government's published plans are to create a stable and proportionate primary assessment system. The changes will support teachers to ensure children gain the necessary skills and knowledge to succeed at secondary school and beyond. Whatever the outcome, you should bear in mind the following when it comes to national tests as we move through the years to come:

There is nothing wrong with teaching to the test as long as the test is a good one.
Primary school children need to practise exam technique.
Completed test papers should always be shared with parents so that they can assist you in the drive towards improved success next time round.
Schools that allow KS1 assessments to be too generous will rue their carelessness when the children are tested at the end of KS2 and progress measures calculated.
Moderation using the 'secure fit' model is wholly inappropriate in terms of reflecting the genuine progress children have made.
Children should be tested termly to monitor progress (no more than that) and a gaps analysis completed on behalf of teachers on each occasion as a result. The analysis must inform future planning.
Evidence must be assembled during the year assiduously if teacher assessments at KS1 and KS2 are to stand up to authority moderation – reference to the exemplification materials must feature in planning and signpost outcomes.

Section 7: Communication

"I know you are in there Mrs Williams!"

An Open Door Policy

The first thing I did when appointed my first headship was to buy something ...

Champagne?

No. A door wedge! (Though, if truth be told, the champagne came shortly afterwards.)

I planned to use the wedge to prop open my office door. It being a fire door, my business manager would raise an eyebrow – but sometimes you have to go out on a limb!

Mine would be an 'open door' headship.

But I would want to add some further stipulations.

I was determined not to be a *'Pop-back-later, I'm-busy-at-the-minute'* Head. I would push things to one side – even if I was snowed under – and make time for that individual who wanted to see me. The word soon got out that I was accessible. My target: never once send someone away. In 20 years of headship, I never have; so it can't be that hard to do – can it?

I once worked with a Head who asked people to make appointments to see him with the diary secretary. And you could wait a week, if not longer. Not the sort of Head, I wanted to be.

And finally, I wanted everyone to know it was an open door. All staff, the parents, the governors and the children.

Someone once said to be the measure of an open door is whether the cleaner feels as comfortable knocking on it as the deputy head; the Y2 child as much as the Y6 child? It was a lesson I didn't want to ever forget.

You know you have an open door when parents or colleagues ask before closing it! That's the litmus test.

What's more...

Those who really have it cracked are those whose office is centrally situated. I never like my office to be tucked away. If you can place yourself at the hub of things, staff get to see you – not to mention the children. I have taken the smaller room to accomplish this. The size of your office comes second to its position.

Managing Relationships with Parents

I have had parents threaten to put me through the window, and I have had parents offer to buy me dining room furniture in appreciation of my efforts. Was I treating either set differently? I like to think not. But context is everything. Sometimes we only see the ugly side of people when there are problems to be sorted. When it's plain sailing, it is easy to be everyone's friend.

If we took the maxim, the customer is always right, and applied it to schools, we might enjoy better relationships with parents but run schools that weren't as good as they could be. Because not all parents know what is best for their children. If I had a pound for every time I have been told, 'I know my son, and he wouldn't lie,' – I'd be a rich man. Parents don't know what their children are capable of as they move through school life independent of them.

I have learnt some important lessons along the way, however:

- never ignore a complaint; it won't go away and procrastination only succeeds in exasperating the complainant
- try not to make knee jerk judgements
- an irate parent is not always best seen there and then – sometimes they need to cool off
- never show temper or irritation, however annoyed or irritated you might be
- stick to the facts and never get personal
- always say that you will need to find out the teacher's version if you do not already know it.

'Know who the nutters are!'

A head teacher colleague said this to me. Speaking as someone with a mental disability – diagnosed OCD – I could have taken offence. I didn't. Life is too short. I think what they meant was – know who your 'vulnerable' parents are – they may be unpredictable. Get to know them – keep them close because it will make them easier to manage.

Outstanding schools know their parents as well as their children.

Newsletters

Newsletters are vital in your efforts to communicate with parents.

Some Dos and Don'ts:

- don't publish attendance tables – they irritate parents and quite rightly. Can illness (and some children are genuinely ill) be rated in a league table?

- do include a Thought for the Week that is highly personal – it will allow parents to relate to you intimately – I reprint one for you below

- key dates – nothing frustrates parents more than not knowing what is going on

- a list of pupils' achievements – parents like this

- avoid Star of the Week – it causes division and dissatisfaction – it becomes whose turn is it this week? – someone has to wait till week 30!

- include things the children have said and done – it will take some work on your part to make it work but it speaks volumes.

Thought for the Week

When was the last time you saw someone with profound learning difficulties? When was the last time you saw a hundred such people gathered in one place? You may never have been in this situation. This week, I was. It was time for Scott, our middle son's annual review at the 'special school' that he attends. As you may recall, Scott is 8 and has autism. After the meeting, Suzanne and I popped into the dining hall to catch him eating his lunch. Each day I come to work with children who can walk and talk and do clever things with numbers and words. To be in a special school where children cannot do these things with ease and confidence is a very humbling experience. To see so many children in one go was rather overwhelming, to be honest. I think it important that all of us with able bodied children take a minute to realise how fortunate we are. That doesn't mean, of course, that we love our darling Scott any less than his able bodied brother and sister. We love him for the person he is, not the person we imagined he was going to be. As I get older, I seem to understand less and less about the world but at the same time I know an awful lot more: one of the things I know is that 'special schools', as we call them, are full of special people. The children within them keep going – in their case – day-in, day-out, usually with laughter and smiles.

Outstanding head teachers are prepared to share their personal stories with other parents.

Parents' Evening

Parents' evenings offer the head teacher a golden opportunity in the space of a short time to make personal contact with every parent whose child attends the school. All you have to do is limit entry to one central point and then plonk yourself there for the duration – you can then go into handshaking mode and personally greet every arrival. This goes a long way.

Parents need to leave parents' evenings clear on what the teacher wanted to say. Some teachers are reluctant to deliver plain messages, especially when they know it will not be what the parent wants to hear. Teachers use all sorts of euphemisms that cloud key information. Children are described as lively or chatty. That's fine if that is what the teacher wants to convey. However, if they mean challenging or disruptive, then they should say so. It does nobody any favours if teachers do not tackle situations openly. Newly qualified teachers will need support with meetings. If you can timetable some meetings before others, allow them to sit in on an experienced teacher meeting with parents. It will be an invaluable opportunity for them to see something modelled that they may never have encountered before.

It is good to give parents something to take away with them. An up-to-date set of improvement targets will do the trick, however only if such targets will be followed through. If they are to be discarded then it is a waste of everyone's time. Far better to set class or group targets that can be monitored.

It is important that staff do not meet with parents in their own classroom alone. It is much better to have the whole year group together in one space or, in a small school, all teachers together positioned around the Hall. Staff can be vulnerable on such evenings in any school and you will want to reduce the risks that come with such 'lone working'.

On parents' evenings, spare a thought for the school's neighbours. It can be difficult living next to a school at the best of times. On parents' evenings driveways can be parked over and garages blocked. If you can open up the playground and use it as a car park, it can be useful. (This is a health and safety consideration in itself however and will certainly require a risk assessment.)

Parent/Teacher Associations

Parent/ Teacher associations exist for two reasons. The first is the obvious one: to raise money for the school. The second is to provide a fulfilling outlet for some parents' energies – some parents greatly enjoy being involved in the organisation and delivery of fund-raising events. I have worked in schools where I needed the money and schools were it has not been so important. Don't make the mistake of thinking it is all about the cash. It is not. Some parents satisfy some inner need by being intimately involved in the running of such organisations. If you don't allow them scope to satisfy those needs, you will hinder relationships with what tend to be more often than not some of your more vocal parent base.

Although heads will be tired at weekends and evenings, it is most important that you show your face at PTA events. Not to do so will earn you a large slice of disrespect. People will say you do not value their efforts to support the children. So don't agree to too many functions as you will not want to disappoint – your work/life balance is important too.

Always take the view that the Parent/Teacher Association should decide where to spend the money they have raised. You can make suggestions, of course. But that is different to taking decisions. It is their money, not yours, and it is a good thing to remember that. Whilst talking about money, it is crucial that the association is properly audited. It is not unheard of for groups to get themselves into financial hot water through perceived irregularities. There is a very effective Parent/ Teacher Association national body and all such associations need to be members.

All PTA events need proper risk assessments undertaken by members of the PTA. These should be available for scrutiny by school management.

Dealing with Difficult People

> **'I want to try to make difficult people somehow relatable.'**
> **Rebecca Hall** (Actress)

You are most certainly going to come across some difficult people.

What drives them?

In my experience, they fall into two camps.

They are either unkind or insecure. Simplistic, I know.

I went on training many years ago that encouraged the delegates to use the four point – one minute – put-down to staff who were proving difficult.

1. Tell them what the problem is.

2. Tell them why you are unhappy about it

3. Say what you expect to happen in the future.

4. Spell out the consequences of inaction

We were encouraged to deliver the above within the minute, counting the four items off on fingers secreted in our pockets.

I tried it for a while. I got quite good at it. It worked, in that I came across as confident and determined. It failed because it was a winner/loser scenario, as outlined by Covey. We should all be striving for win/win scenarios according to this guru. I'm not sure win/win is always possible – I think you have to be extremely talented to deliver that – but there is no mileage in making your point and leaving the other person feeling bitter and dejected. This will just add to their status amongst your staff as a malcontent, hell bent on contradicting your every initiative. I think sometimes the best we can hope for when challenged aggressively is 'I almost won/ you certainly didn't lose.'

The best approach that I have discovered is to use the less confrontational,

'When you say/ do this, it makes me feel...'

Sometimes, just sometimes, the person you are confronting (for want of a better word) hasn't considered the situation from your view point. Sadly, sometimes, they indeed have and you are just going to have to disappoint them by asserting yourself. And asserting yourself is what you are going to have to do. That doesn't mean you have to take up every challenge that a difficult person sets you – some you can let go – keeping your powder dry – living to fight another day. When I was first a Head, I was 'a last word' freak; I always had to have it. My advice is to chill out. Assert yourself when it matters but let the trivia pass you by – like logs floating down the river. You'll keep your sanity and enjoy your job more.

Beware the member of staff who has announced their retirement or resignation. Many go with good grace; however, it would be fair to say in my experience that many like to say that things 'ain't what they were' and will purposely go about ruining what they can in the time they have left. Don't rise to the bait. They will be gone soon enough and you will only regret it, if you come down to their level.

Who is best placed to deal with difficult people anyway?

You could argue that the Head should only do it as a last resort. If you have the right people around you, it is far better that they do it. They will learn and grow in so doing. This isn't a cop-out. You will have done your fair share when a deputy. It means you can maintain positive relations with all, with you only becoming involved when others have tried and failed and your intervention is unavoidable.

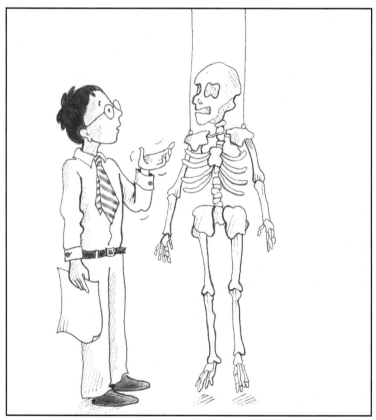

'And let me tell you, things aren't what they used to be!'

Channels of Staff Communication

Outstanding schools have excellent systems of communication.

There are many ways that schools seek to communicate with staff. Things change so quickly – by the hour! Systems of communication must be able to cope. I offer the following model as one that has worked well in a large primary that was judged to be outstanding.

Leadership Teams

Leadership Teams can usefully meet first thing on a Monday to go through the diary for the week. Then again last thing at the end of the week – yes on a Friday after school! – where they can review their weeks – ensuring key news is communicated – and bringing issues to the table so group solutions can be found.

Staff Briefings

Staff can usefully meet on a Monday at the end of the day, prior to the traditional staff training, for a whole staff briefing. A briefing should not be a discussion. If matters need to be discussed other opportunities need to be found. A briefing simply informs staff of what is going to be happening in the week to come. It is good practice to follow it up with a briefing note, so key messages are reinforced and those staff who were unable to attend the briefing – through sickness etc, – are kept in the loop. By writing down what you have said you will have an audit trail – important for when people say they were not told something when you know they were.

Surgeries

All groups of staff – administrative, maintenance, teachers and teaching assistants – should have a termly surgery where they have an opportunity to comment on what is going well and what could be improved. I am including for you the proforma we use in our school as a starting point to developing your own.

Once the surgery is complete, the Leadership Team can together consider points raised and find group solutions to problems and concerns. The Leadership Team's response to the surgeries should then be published to all.

Emails

Try to resist the temptation to communicate by email. That's fine if you work for LEGO and have in excess of a hundred colleagues but, in a primary school, the personal touch is usually appreciated so seek your colleagues out. Emails and briefing notes are useful, however, when you want an audit trail of communication you have shared. This guards against the colleague who likes to say, 'Nobody told me...'

St. Bede's Staff Surgery

Teachers and Teaching Assistants		Administration		Maintenance	

Standing Agenda

Health and Safety including security (issues arising)	
Training (Recently undertaken or needed)	
Stress Awareness To whom would I raise concerns?	
Direction of the School Clarity? Agreement?	
Following Policies Are we?	
Child Protection (Have any concerns been properly processed? Do we know?)	
What went well this half term?	
What could have gone better this half term?	
AOB	

Phase Leader .... Signed ....

Key Messages: 20 sound bites

> 'We printed our key characteristics on to sheets of plastic and put them up in corridors. It kept us focussed.'
>
> **Governor**

I offer 20 characteristics here for your careful consideration in your first year of headship. You could get some of them printed on to boards that could be displayed around the corridors and staff room.

> **Outstanding schools constantly repeat their key messages.**

- Leaders who ask 'So what?' more than 'What next?'
- Subject leaders who shape curricula as much as evaluate them
- Deputies who lead as well as they manage
- Governors who support as much as they challenge
- Chairs of Governors who are pragmatic rather than dogmatic
- Governors who insist their challenge is recorded in the minutes of meetings
- Business managers who watch the pence as much as they watch the pounds
- Teachers who ask the next question
- ... and the one after that
- Teachers who ask 'why' more than 'what'
- Teachers who insist that there should be demonstrable progress in every, not just most, lessons
- Teachers who follow through in their marking
- Colleagues who see reading as the cornerstone of all learning
- Learning assistants who extend as much as consolidate
- Children who question their peers as much as their teachers
- Classrooms where children are independent
- Classrooms where children do more talking than the adults
- Parents who feel sufficiently informed to ask the right questions
- Parents who are equipped to support their children's learning
- Assemblies that touch the soul.

Mind Your Language

'There is nothing worse than hearing a colleague talk down to children – far better to stretch them with words they have yet to meet. There has to be a first time.'

English Advisor

You have a key role to play in ensuring that the language you use to children is equally demanding and supportive. As lead communicator in the school, you will need to have high expectations of the language to which your pupils should be exposed. The thing that makes me cringe above all others is to see a head teacher using language in assembly that is well within the grasp of the pupils. It should instead stretch them at every turn.

The children may not be able to explain the meaning of the words you use (a skill in itself) but they may understand them in context and, if you are in any doubt, back-up what you say with a different phrasing of the same idea. This will stretch them and enable their own vocabularies to grow.

I offer here some words that children should be exposed to – in context – during assembly time:

9-11 year olds	features, represent, original, characteristics, dominate, source, chaos, problematic, functions, decade, personality, extreme, limits, optional, priority, crucial, anonymous, absolute, abundant, bewilder, biased, postpone, credit, border, critical, fascinate, glaring, headline, impudent, ignite, jury, knowledgeable, league, literally, limit, minority, navigate, nocturnal, ominous, perceptive, racist, sacrifice, sarcastic, solution, toxic, topical, current, ultimate, vary, wasteful
7-9 year olds	enthusiasm, characters, difficulty, several, route, modern, destination, judge, ability, benefit, cancel, country, creep, direction, difficult, difference, fantastic, ghastly, helpful, hurtle, jungle, knowledge, liar, lively, main, majority, nervous, one-way, peak, raise, shatter, solid, trade, unbelievable, venom, warrior, volunteer

I could go on and on...

The examples are just that, examples. I could easily have chosen from hundreds more.

Some colleagues will be surprised at the level of difficulty I am advocating. I make no apologies. The research is clear. Middle class children hear far more words and a wider range of words than children in receipt of welfare payments – Hart and Risley (2003–8) found that a pre-school child on welfare hears 616 words per hour as compared with the 2,153 heard by the child in a middle class home. Studies have shown that language acquisition is key to future academic success and the head teacher must push, push and then push some more. If they are not hearing it at home, they need to hear it at school. Sadly, they won't be hearing it as often as you would like in all classrooms – some teachers talk down to children and you will need to tackle this – but in the meantime they must hear it in assembly and whenever encountering you.

Visitors to School

There are bound to be some of these during your first year. Be cautious!

The best intentioned of visitors can quickly whip an assembled school into a state of frenzy. The majority think that as some children like to scream and shout, that is the way to go. Thought provoking reflection is often not on the agenda, sadly. Many will appeal to the lowest common denominator. It will be your job to bring the children back down to earth and send them back to class ready to learn.

Beware of visiting authors most of all. They can be an invaluable way of getting the children interested in both reading and writing. I have enjoyed many inspirational presentations. However, such visitors will vary in quality so a recommendation from other colleagues is worth a great deal. Some will use all sorts of naughty words in an attempt to get the audience on side and do risqué things. I once had one who finished his routine with a school 'burping' competition. The shame of it!

Relationships with Other Schools

It is very useful to foster good working relationships with other schools. These may be local schools or those further afield – similar to your school in context, or different. The more variety you can establish, the better. Lots of schools find they gain particularly from establishing links with schools in similar settings. You can only learn from such experiences. Apart from the usual sporting and musical events, nowhere is this collaboration more important than when talking about pupils' work in order to agree common standards being achieved by different children in different schools. It seems likely that such cross-school moderation can only become more important in the ever changing world of primary assessment.

The most difficult relationship that exists in education circles is that between infant and junior head teachers. How so? The simple fact of the matter is that junior heads will be judged upon the value they add to KS1 results. How is this different, you ask, to how the secondary school head is judged? Well the secondary head is judged upon the value added to externally marked test results at age 11; whereas, the junior head is judged upon the value that they are judged to have added to teacher assessments at the age of 7. There is a world of difference. The all through primary head has at least some control. Their teachers assess the standard of children on entry to Reception and at the end of Key Stage 1; they can stand or fall on the outcomes at KS2, knowing that their destiny – was to some degree – in their own hands. Junior Heads must have an excellent relationship with their feeder infant school. Never talk about over inflated results. It will antagonise. Instead put your energies into sharing together pupils' work from both schools and attempting to agree upon the standards that such scrutiny suggests.

Dealing with the Media

There are many opportunities to engage positively with the local media. Local papers are invariably interested in school stories, which can promote the school to the wider community and even attract prospective parents. Try to gain some control over how the story is presented; some reporters will be happy to share the article with you prior to publication, which can avoid the potential for any misunderstanding. Clearly permission to use images of children and their names must be secured in writing from parents.

However, nothing gets directors of local authorities or MAT CEOs more agitated than unwelcome involvement of the press in school matters. Always, always involve the local authority or Trust PR team. Don't deal with the press directly yourself in contentious matters. I have had national and local media involved in school controversies and not a year goes by without a head teacher gaining unwelcome headlines. As I write a head teacher has hit the headlines for cancelling a nativity so her Y2 pupils could focus on SATs. I am sure that is not what happened but it is always worth bearing in mind the potential for a story being misrepresented.

Front of House

What your Reception area says about you is oh so important. So why do so many schools get it wrong? It is not a doctor's surgery where a brusque receptionist keeps the patients at bay. The role of the school receptionist is different. They are required to be confidante, information point and wise counsel. Many parents will judge the school – and therefore you – upon the quality of reception they receive from the front of office staff. Get this right and it will serve you well. Get it wrong and you will forever be on the back foot. Don't get office staff to serve as a barrier between you and parents. If an irate parent wants to speak to you on the phone, don't encourage the office team to report that you are 'in a meeting' – even if you are. Instead have them say they will ask you to phone them at their earliest opportunity. The secretary's job is then to get as much information for you so you come to the conversation forearmed. Secretaries who are overzealous can make matters worse – it gets parents' backs up – and don't always believe what you are being told about how a parent has presented on the phone. Be your own judge and give the parent the benefit of the doubt until you have spoken to them personally.

Complaints Policy

I like it when the school has the more rounded 'Compliments and Complaints' Policy. It is a more positive approach than just having a complaints procedure, although it is a requirement that you have the latter. If a parent has a complaint, then they need to know what to do. Any policy must be clearly written. It is very easy to take complaints personally, especially when they are written or delivered in a personal manner. This does not get easier. We instinctively react in a defensive way when challenged. Deal with all complaints professionally and objectively. It is always a good idea to respond quickly to written complaints – as soon as you know what it is you want to say and have checked your facts.

What should you do if a group of disgruntled parents come calling? Be brave and see them together. It may not be pleasant but you lose respect when you say you will only see complainants one at a time.

Assemblies

Assemblies are key. They are your weekly opportunity to make contact with children and staff. Although staff and children can legally withdraw from an act of worship, very few do. For ten minutes or so, you have an opportunity to make your mark. However, there are some associated problems.

Firstly, it is the head teacher's responsibility to ensure that there is a daily act of worship. They can take different settings – class, phase or whole school based. But the regulations (Education Act 1998) are clear: assemblies must be broadly Christian in nature. That's fine in the shires but more problematic in some inner city schools where two thirds of the children if not more may be of a different faith. What then? I recently led a school that was two-thirds Muslim. The guidance says that to be broadly Christian, there must be some reference to Jesus. Although some of the world's religions recognise Jesus as a religious figure, some do not. Too many schools opt out altogether and make their assemblies exclusively secular – sometimes with a reflection rather than a prayer to finish; however, in so doing they do not meet the requirements of the Act and if it is only done when OFSTED come calling, the inspectors may see the inconsistency. It is of course worth remembering that the Act only says that the majority of the acts of worship need to be thus characterised. That leaves plenty of scope to reflect the stories of other faiths elsewhere. That said, schools can apply to their local Standing Advisory Council on Religious Education (SACRE) board for a 'determination' if they wish to gain exemption from delivering broadly Christian assemblies. If granted, a 'full determination' permits the school's daily worship to be based upon a religion other than Christianity: whereas, a 'part determination' permits collective worship to be varied to suit other religions.

Secondly, there is a dearth of good assembly material on the market. You want stories: stories that will make the children laugh, cry and think. When I was first a Head I bought every single collection of assembly stories on the market. I found I could only use one or two of the stories that were contained within each volume. It was expensive and disappointing. I therefore decided to write my own. I based my stories on events that had happened in my school. You could do the same. Also, try those of Michael Catchpool and Pat Lunt – these are quality tales.

In the absence of good stories for assemblies, Heads have filled their assemblies with presentations of awards, certificates and sharing of good work. However, nothing connects with children like the telling of a good story.

Class-led assemblies are hugely enjoyable for everyone – staff, children and parents. But they take time and effort and you won't want to ask your teachers to present more than one a year.

There should also be music to welcome the children in and leave. This is an opportunity to expose the children to the full range of types of music. The temptation is to play something classical – but there is modern music, world music, jazz, funk – a whole world out there. I find movie sound tracks often set the right tones for the ten minutes or so of reflection that will follow. The sound tracks to Gladiator and Castaway can be used for the assembly that you have to get just right – the one when 'visitors' join the audience.

And you should sometimes consider using a prayer rather than a secular pause for reflection. Children should be invited to pray, rather than told to pray. Just pray to God; you don't have to specify which God. In this way you can be inclusive, with children choosing whether they wish to join you or not.

I include a story here for you. I hope you enjoy it. My children tell me they did.

Dan and Simon's Story (An assembly story for children)

Dan and Simon were good friends. It was Dan, who discovered tennis first. He introduced Simon to the game one Saturday morning on the local courts. Both boys took to the game and grasped the fundamentals bit by bit. Then just as they were getting started, the autumn arrived and tennis rackets were put away with footballs retrieved from the garden shed.

The boys' parents had picked up on the summer fun, and both Simon and Dan received new tennis rackets for Christmas; they were looking forward to the new season. With the brighter days of March the boys took to the courts again. They were to have lessons from Hal, the local club's coach. Young and friendly, it was easy to work hard for Hal. Dan had to put extra effort into his serve, which was weaker than that of his friend. He couldn't quite get the ball toss right: if he threw it too low, he had to cramp his shoulders to meet the ball in time, invariably hitting it into the net; whereas if he threw it too high, he mis-timed his swing and ended up hitting it long. Would he ever get the hang of it? Simon meanwhile was having trouble with his backhand. Hal, the coach, told him to picture dealing whilst playing pontoon – the natural way to do that was backhanded when the opponent decided to twist. Simon thought he understood but he couldn't help feeling it was complicated. But both boys worked hard. After school each day, they made their way to the practice courts for an hour before tea. There were other kids there too, of course. Many of them were more naturally gifted then either Dan or Simon. Things seem to come so easy to them. However, rather than being de-motivated by this, it just seemed to spur the boys on: the better the other kids played, the harder the two friends worked. They would stay longer on the practice courts than the other kids. Dan's serve improved and so did Simon's backhand.

As they approached the summer holidays, Hal announced that there was to be a club championship. There would be gold, silver and bronze medals, just like at the Olympics. There was a buzz in the changing rooms at Saturday morning lessons. Carl Simpkins, who fancied himself rotten, was busy holding court when the two boys arrived to change.

'And remember,' Carl said, 'winners come first, not second or third.' Whilst some of the boys loudly agreed with him, the remainder stayed quiet. Carl was a big boy and nobody wanted to take him on, especially in front of an audience.

On the way home, Dan was the first to mention it. 'What about this championship?, he ventured. 'Do you think we should enter?' Carl's words rang in Simon's ears, 'Winners come first, not second or third.'

'Well', he said, 'one thing's for sure, we're not going to win.' Both boys knew there were players who were bigger and better than they.

'We have nothing to lose, do we?' said Dan. 'Nobody will expect anything of us, why not?

The two boys decided to put their names forward. When they gave their competition entries to Hal, he seemed genuinely pleased. They had worked hard he said, so deserved their place.

The following Saturday the seeding for the tournament were announced. In tennis you were seeded, ranked in other words, so that the best players could be kept apart to the semi-finals and finals. There were sixteen pairs of boys entered in the tournament. Dan and Simon looked at the list that had been pinned up to the notice board. They were bottom, sixteenth – no surprise there – and in the very first round they would play Jonathan Masters and Clive Pickles. They were quite a pair.

There were two weeks before the championship would begin and it would be played over a fortnight, the final being on the last Sunday, preceded on the same afternoon by the third place play off. The boys practised for over two hours after school on Monday and at the end of the session, Simon felt a painful twinge in his elbow. When he got home, his mother was concerned and took him to see the GP. By then he could hardly straighten his elbow without pain.

'Hmmn,' said Dr Jacobs, 'you have either been washing lots of windows or playing too much tennis. Which is it?' Simon grinned.

'Tennis, Doctor,' he said. 'It's much more fun that washing windows' – not that he had ever washed any, his mother chipped in.

'Well, you have two choices. No more tennis, or a rather painful injection into the elbow. Then with a week's rest, you should be okay.

Simon felt winded – all that work and effort, not to play in the championships. But to his mother's surprise, he chose the injection. It hurt, and then it hurt some more. He rested for a week and then took to the practice courts again. It was better; a little sore, but definitely better.

The day of their first match arrived. For some unfathomable reason, Dan was nervous. Like he had been before his SATS last summer. It wasn't a test: it was meant to be fun – so why should he feel like that?

The first set was gone in a flash. The boys lost it 6–1. Clive in particular hit the ball so hard. But then in the second both Simon and Dan seemed to find their rhythm. Individually, neither of them was as good as Clive or Jonathan, but together they were a better team. They had spent so many months on the practice courts that they seemed to know where their partner was and what they would do next. They won the set 7–5. Clive, they could tell was angry and in the third and deciding set his temper – which had always been quite strong – boiled over. He hit the ball harder and harder but started to miss the lines with the ball sailing out. Much to their surprise and to Clive and Jonathan's amazement, Simon and Dan won the third set and with it the match 6–3. The two friends were over the moon. Hal too was delighted. 'You're by no means the best players at the club,' he said, 'but you work so hard in training. You deserve it. Now stay calm. On paper, you have an easier match next. Win it and you're in the semi-finals. And win it they did, in straight sets 7–5 7–5.

The boys couldn't believe it, they were in the semi-finals. One match from the finals. The only problem they were playing Miles and his partner Lucas. Parents and friends were courtside to watch the match. Could the two friends do it? They lost the first set 6–0. Miles and Lucas were in a different league. Not only did they hit the ball hard but they were accurate too. In the second set, the boys did manage to get on the scoreboard but lost the match 6–0 6–2. It was embarrassing. Their bubble had been well and truly burst. Miles and Lucas would be in the final, not them.

Hal was great.

'You gave it your best,' he said. 'I'm proud of you. Still a chance of a medal tomorrow. Someone will win the bronze in the third and fourth place play-off. It could be you. But both the boys were dejected. They stayed in the changing room, towels over their heads, wanting the floor to swallow them up. In walked Miles. The boys glanced out from under their towels and inwardly groaned. What was he going to say to them?

'Just one thing boys,' he said smirking, 'winners come first, not second or third.'

It was a killer punch and all three boys knew it.

The day of the bronze medal match dawned early. They were up against Charlie and Ryan, the fifth seeds. No way could they win that, they knew it. Hal saw them before the match.

'Don't you go into the match, thinking you have lose before you even begin. If you do, you will have. Go out there and enjoy it. You've done brilliantly to get this far. Everyone is talking about you.'

Were they? wondered the boys.

Could they win it?

They would certainly try.

The first set was surprisingly close and Dan and Simon narrowly lost it on a tie-break 7–6. The second was closer still but now the boys were growing in confidence and they won it again on a tie breaker. The third set started well for them when they broke Charlie's serve. Charlie was annoyed and first he swore, then he smashed his racket on the floor. He got a warning for that. Dan and Simon were inwardly pleased. Were their opponents about to crack? Before they knew it the boys were 4–1 up, just two games from victory and the bronze medal. Dan suddenly felt nervous again. He looked at Simon, who ran over to his friend.

'Stay calm,' he said, 'we can win this.'

The boys took the next game, it was 5–1. One game from the magical six that would win them the set, the match and the bronze medal.

Simon, ran over again. 'I know,' said Dan, 'we are going to win it.'

And win it they did, 6–2.

The boys were elated. Their families were thrilled; Dan's mum was even crying.

The final was played next and Miles and Lucas won gold.

As the boys were changing in the dressing room, everyone bundled in keen to congratulate the winners. To Dan and Simon's surprise, it was them that everyone wanted to talk to, not Miles. There were pats on the back, cheers and handshakes. 'But we didn't come first,' said Dan, surprised by this reaction. 'No,' said Hal, 'but yours was the greater victory. Everyone expected Miles to win but nobody – and I mean nobody – expected you two to get bronze. All that training and hard work certainly paid off. You may not have been the best players, but you've worked harder than anyone else.'

Dan looked up at a moody looking Miles.

'See,' Dan said,' winners do come third!'

Section 8: Finance

It is frightening how it all adds up...

Managing Money

Your role will be to decide with others how money should be spent and then to ensure you stay within budget. It will be the role of the business manager or bursar to process the payments. School budgets are dominated by staff salaries and there will generally be little money for you to play with. This makes your job more difficult, not less: everyone will be asking you for money for one thing or another as you progress through the year. You must learn to disappoint people if you cannot see any likely gain for children's learning and even then only to agree if you know – not you think – you can afford it.

It is important you plan ahead and involve governors closely in the financial strategic direction of the school. These are not decisions for you to make on your own. You will have an agreed sum that you can spend without having to make reference to the Governors, usually £10,000 or thereabouts. But larger budgets must be agreed by them. My advice is to always plan for three years: you need to move forward with your gaze very much up rather than down. Pay particular attention to the incremental rises that staff will expect in pay. The same team may cost you a very different sum in three years' time. Given that wages dominate budgets, this is crucial.

You will want to give your subject leaders a sum of money to spend on their subject areas. Keep it small but then let them spend it; don't interfere with their choices. Your school action plan must be funded. You will need to allocate sums to each area for improvement. But remember that many improvements do not cost money. They simply require you to move forward differently.

In terms of cost centres, you must ensure that the fabric of the building is maintained – there should be a rolling programme – and that you have enough money in teacher insurances and cover supply to enable you to deal with unexpected staffing issues that arise – the sudden departure of a member of staff with a more expensive replacement or the long-term absence of a member of staff due to illness or maternity. I always like to have a 5% contingency sum each year to allow for the many unexpected events that can come your way. And come your way, they will!

Keep a keen eye on how money is being spent in accordance with your agreed budgets. Never let a month pass by when you don't sit down with your school business manager and consider overspends and underspends. Then do this with governors – a meeting each month with the finance sub-committee is worth its weight in gold. Call it the Finance and General Purposes committee and you are guaranteed a slot once a month where you can bring other matters arising to the governors' attention.

Learn to benchmark yourself against other schools who are getting better outcomes than you with the same resources. Visit some of these schools if you can and see how they spend their money in action.

Best value is something that should infuse every large financial decision you take. And remember, best value does not mean cheapest. Be sure of the service you are being offered and ensure that there is a means of raising dissatisfaction before you sign on the dotted line.

All schools work within checks and balances that are aimed at ensuring public money is spent appropriately. When you have your first independent audit, expect there to be shortcomings. There nearly always are. Do not be downhearted. Quickly set about outing them right and involve governors each step of the way.

You do not want a deficit budget. That said, it is surprising how many schools have them. No, you want to be in surplus. This is easier said than done when budgets are getting increasingly tight but is often achievable, if you cut your cloth accordingly. The problem with some schools is that they have historically punched above their weight where finance is concerned – they have quite simply spent too much. If your staff is too expensive, you must look to make it cheaper as you work your way through the resignations and subsequent appointments that will come your way. A less expensive staff does not necessarily mean a less effective one. You will want to skew your staff in the direction of lesser experienced colleagues, who are cheaper and often just as effective. How big should your carry forward be? Not so big as to gain unwanted attention; and you must be mindful that the year's allocation is meant to be spent on the current cohorts of children at your school. But you do want a reasonable carry forward. It will give you a contingency and ensure you can sleep at night.

Do not let your school waste money. Many do. For example, the amount that schools spend on ink and paper only to see things discarded once printed is a concern. There is an old maxim, 'Take care of the pennies and the pounds will take care of themselves.' There is much truth in that. It is not your job to watch the pennies; however, it your job to appoint people who will.

The days of local authorities providing services to schools are diminishing rapidly, although some are going down with a fight. Most maintained schools find themselves in no different a place than academies or free schools: they select providers for school services from a range of commercial providers. Recommendations are important.

One final note in all financial matters, be transparent. Never do anything personally or professionally that would lay you open to criticism. You must be squeaky clean. The media is full of stories where the spending of public money is called into doubt.

Section 9:
Safeguarding and Health and Safety

Safeguarding

There is a fine line between keeping confidences and ensuring that people know about issues that may be affecting a child's behaviour and well-being. In my own school, children who have had Social Care involvement or worked with other agencies have a red folder. Teachers of those children have access to that file, as do child protection officers. I would never want to be in the position when a teacher could say to me,' I didn't know that I should have been alert to something.'

It will be important to have a simple system which allows staff (any staff) to flag up a welfare concern regarding a child. In our school, it is a simple Record of Concern (ROC) form that we have devised and use. They are always shared with me – the Child Protection Officer for the school – and I record any action that I have taken upon them.

See page 158 for a simple ROC (Record of Concern)

Record of Concern

Date ....

Child's Name ....

Class..

Concern

Completed by ....

Form shared with...

Time...

Follow Up From Safeguarding Lead

Outside Agencies Involved

Signed ....

Date ....

Follow up shared as appropriate

Security

It is an uncomfortable truth that no school is a citadel. If someone is really determined to get in, they will. What you need to ensure is that you have sufficient red flags to deter them: doors that only open from the inside; CCTV; key pad/ fob entry systems; name badges for all staff and visitors. A culture of closing doors after you and staff challenging people without a badge. If you are unfortunate enough to have an intruder, let parents know. You will want to tell them how it was possible and what you intend to do about it. Ensure security is a standing agenda item on governing body meetings and staff surgeries.

Health and Safety

There are very few things that are going to get you into the dock, as a head teacher. Though it might not seem like it, poor SAT results aren't one of them!

There are some criminal acts but those are likely to trouble very few. More will be troubled, however, by breeches of Health and Safety.

It is important that risk assessments are in place. They need to cover each aspect of school life where there is a perceived risk. And they need to be accessible, used and regularly reviewed.

In addition, you will need termly inspections of the building and your assessments by a third party. Trained governors can fulfil this role but an LA representative would be better, though they may undertake such inspections less frequently and want to be paid. However, health and safety is more than a set of risk assessments and inspections – important though they are. Rather it is a way of being, a culture where risks are identified, communicated and then controlled or eliminated by everyone in the school – from the cleaner to the head teacher.

Always ensure routine inspections and maintenance checks are up-to date. The list is endless – air conditioning, lightning conductors, fire extinguishers etc. Delegate, but keep tabs on this important area of school life! And always ensure that combustible materials don't gather anywhere in mounds of clutter! Don't allow clutter anywhere in your school! It's like letting a teenager live with a messed up bedroom; easy to do but far easier to regret...

A quick and handy approach is to design a risk assessment review sheet. If nothing has changed – the same risks and controls are identified – you don't need to write a new risk assessment. Just note that there has been no change and sign and date. Never create work for the sake of it and certainly not in this aspect of school life, which will grow like Topsy given the opportunity. I reproduce a review sheet that we currently use in our school.

RISK ASSESSMENT ANNUAL REVIEW

A	Risk Assessment Name		Dated	Date of Review
B	Any additional hazards not already identified			
			YES	NO
C	Any additional persons at risk			
			YES	NO
D	Are the control measures in place working			
			YES	NO

Notes

If you have answered Yes to question B or C, you must record the changes on the risk assessment form.

If you have answered No to question D, a full review of the risk assessment will need to be made and additional control measures considered.

If you have reviewed the risk assessment and there are no changes or you have not completed the actions required on the risk assessment you may wish to make comments in section E below.

E	Comments	Action date and by whom	
F	Has a new risk assessment been produced as a result of this review?	Yes	No
Signed		Date	

Section 10: When Things Go Wrong

Expect the Unexpected

'Nothing to me is unexpected. No disappointment is unexpected – whether it's movies or people or relationships. I'm always ready for the punch directly between the eyes. So I get hurt, but I never get hurt. Happens all the time.'

Brian Grazer (Film and Television Producer)

Nothing is going to protect you from the unexpected. Not experience, not luck. I have been doing the job for 20 years now and I have had to deal with a number of unexpected events; I list some for you below. I am just as likely to meet a new one as you are.

- flood of the main building;
- death of a child;
- break-in;
- missing child;
- slashed tyre whilst parked in the car park;
- poison pen letter from colleague;
- tears;
- windows blown out by local gas explosion;
- fire;
- teacher's anti-government blog going viral;
- interview of said teacher on BBC;
- staff member having a seizure in assembly;
- caretaker kissing a cleaner in his room;
- more tears;
- death of a parent;
- child posting an indecent image of themselves on social media
- child cheating in SATS with mobile;
- fire alarm going off (unintentionally);
- NQTs being romantically involved and consequently over familiar in the corridor;
- staff mutiny;
- parent petition;
- parent punching another parent;
- parent slapping a teacher;
- yet more tears;
- child going home with a teacher's car keys;
- parent expecting to high-five you;

- member of staff suffering from manic depression having an episode in class;
- teaching assistant taking a colleague's medication and having to be helped off the premises and home;
- teacher coming out as gay whilst working in a Catholic school;
- child with Tourettes swearing in assembly;
- child with OCD, pooing on the floor because the toilet seat was contaminated;
- death of a member of staff – on and off the premises;
- child alleging parent hits them with a belt;
- head teacher falling in love with and marrying one of the teachers;
- parent removing a child permanently without the other parent's knowledge;
- teacher out drinking when meant to be on a course;
- child with offending haircut appearing on front page of local paper following internal exclusion;
- parent ordering 30 bed pans from local health centre because they alleged teacher wasn't allowing children to use the toilet;
- staff member drunk on the premises;
- member of staff arrested for possession of a class A drug;
- discovery of asbestos panels in the main building;
- boiler breakdown leading to school closure;
- missing parent;
- parent out for dinner rather than collecting child after residential;
- parents involved in wife swap;
- teacher on mobile in class during walk round by the Director;
- male member of staff entering girls' dormitories unaccompanied during residential;
- teacher stripping down to his boxers on a residential;
- parent saying he knew people who could come to school and harm a child;
- member of staff involved in fraudulent mileage claims.

Nothing can protect you from the unexpected. However, how you deal with such scenarios is crucial. Whatever you are feeling on the inside, you must project an image of calm serenity. Staff don't like head teachers who panic. Panic in private, in public remain measured. It's an act, like so much else that we are asked to do. The word you want your staff to use about you is unflappable.

Know People Will Disappoint You

You can expect just a handful of people never to disappoint you. Everyone else will have the propensity to do things of which you would not have thought them capable. It won't matter how long you have known them. The trick is not to feel deflated by such episodes but rather see them as inevitable and most importantly not to take them personally. They would have disappointed another head teacher in your shoes in just the same way. Accept that and you can move on – safe in the knowledge that whilst there will be a next time, you will come through that disappointment just as you have this one.

Section 11: What Next?

"What can I be certain of?"

What Does The Future Hold?

> 'You need to remember to look up from time to time; it is easy to get bogged down in the here and now.'
>
> **Local Education Advisor**
> **Multi Academy Trusts (MATS)**

'Get aboard a train or be told which train you are boarding!' was the stark message I received at a recent conference led by one of the regional commissioners. With the seemingly established demise of Local Education Authorities, we now seem to have academisation by stealth. Be in no doubt, the recent U-turn by the government in terms of forced academisation seems a delaying tactic rather than a change in policy. It seems that it is the government's desire that all schools are academies by 2022.

If you are thinking of applying for the headship of an academy, you will need to pay particular attention to the fine print – namely the academy or trust's terms and conditions of employment and its capability procedure. It may well be different to what you may be offered in the maintained sector. By different, I mean less forgiving. Being a head teacher is a precarious role: none of us is ever far away from a potential dip in pupil results. You will need to assure yourself that your employer realises that the context of any such a dip year will be understood for what it is. It may not mean that you have underperformed that year. It may, it may not.

The CEO

The advent of the CEO of the MAT is a direct threat (and I chose my words carefully) to the autonomy of the head teacher that has existed since the introduction of LMS – Local Management of Schools, for those of you too young to recognise the acronym. Prior to these heady days, a head teacher would have to seek authority from the LEA (Local Education Authority) to have a new tap fitted. How we approach this challenge moving forward will redefine headship.

Coasting

One to watch. The definition will change year on year, it would seem. At the moment, we have a rather generous progress measure which stops a swathe of schools that are below the 85% meeting national expectations benchmark from falling into this category. But if the government grows bolder, the numbers of schools judged to be coasting may grow.

National Funding Formula

The proposed changes seem likely to see some winners and losers; although I would wish to argue that change is long overdue in this area. Some will see it as an opportunity to bemoan the paucity of funding and claim this is no more than shifting deckchairs on the decks of the Titanic.

At the End Of Your First Year

Well if you have survived, you will want to know from your team – teaching and support – how you have done. There are all sorts of questionnaires you can give them to gauge the mood. OFSTED provide one as do others. I prefer the simple one below. However, if you distribute it you have to be prepared for some criticism that will emerge through its completion. It invites it, so you must be prepared to receive it. Go on take the plunge.

What am I doing that you want me to continue doing?

What am I doing that you want me to do differently?

What do you want me to start doing?

What do you want me to stop doing?

Some Quick Dos and Don'ts

You can have an inner circle as a Head, but don't make it obvious!

Most leaders have colleagues within the group whom they rely upon more than others. I have a leadership team of nine, but I rely upon three more than the other six. Never let the others catch on or you will go from talk of inner circle to favourites and marginalisation. Messy!

Know your mind but don't be stubborn

Nothing breeds a lack of confidence in a leader as much as indecision. That doesn't mean arrogance. You can get round that by being honest with others about your faults and mistakes. But people like people who are paid to make decisions to make them.

Be innovative but not a maverick

This will come with time. You can't expect to be innovative too early on in your career. However, it needs to come and it can only come if you are prepared to think outside the box. Don't always rely on others' ideas to shape your school's improvement. Try to think of your own ideas – it will go a long way. Don't however, be a maverick. A maverick is a chancer, someone who may set off with half-baked ideas. Think it through before you launch it and try to cover every eventuality.

Buy educational books but don't let them gather dust like recipe books in a kitchen!

A decent course in London will set your school back around £400. That sum will buy you all the latest books published in a year. You can develop tenfold by reading these – even if its skim reading. John Maxwell says, 'Leaders are readers.' I agree. My two favourites of the last ten years!

Will Ryan – 'Leadership with a Moral Purpose'

Andy Griffith and Mark Burns – Engaging Learners

Buy them and then read them!

Keep your School Evaluation Form (SEF) up to date

Put aside a day every half-term for it. If you fall behind, it becomes very difficult to catch-up. And assemble boxes too that house the evidence that the SEF refers to and cross-reference them. It will be worth it when the OFSTED call comes through. You will have the evidence to hand when you are in panic mode! And don't forget about it once OFSTED have been. You can't take a year out! They will be back before you know it.

Always be prepared to apologise

That sounds obvious I know, good manners, courteous behaviour. But I mean more than that. Be prepared to accept blame – to apologise – even when you believe you are not at fault. If it is going to move the situation forward, just do it. Be the bigger person!

Always leave people room to manoeuvre

There is no point backing someone into a corner. If you don't leave them an exit route in a dispute or argument, they will lose face and resent you. How will that enable you to move forward together? There is a great story told about JFK. In the middle of the Cuban crisis he had sent his ultimatum to the Russians to turn back or else. No response came. Panic set in. Then some bright spark suggested they act as if they had never sent the first ultimatum, but instead send a second, as if for the first time. The Russians turned back. I don't know if the story is true but it illustrates the point rather well. Leave people with a way out.

Be succinct

I don't know if this is true either but I read that Ronald Reagan would never consider anything unless it could be written on two sides of A4. I rather hope it is a true story. I find it encouraging. If a president of the USA could discuss world peace in those terms, we should be able to consider most of the topics that come our way as a school staff within similar parameters.

Never work from home

Teaching colleagues can't do it, so neither should you. Similarly, banish all thought of sabbaticals from your mind; they will also lose you credibility. Staff don't get this luxury, why should you?

Be the first to arrive and last to leave

That doesn't mean there can't be exceptions to the rule. But it is a useful maxim to adopt. Staff don't want to feel that they are working harder than you. You get paid more.

Don't bite

There will be times when people try your patience. They may be unfair, mean spirited or just plain ignorant. Never bite. By bite, I mean, come down to their level. Any sense of satisfaction you feel for speaking your mind will quickly fade. And they may bite back!

Be prepared to work each evening and throughout the weekend

Yes, you need time off but this is a hard job. You asked to do it. And if you don't intend to do this, don't tell your staff! They will assume you do as many of them have to in order to deliver the quality they strive for.

Make sure you are seen out of your office

No one wants a head holed up in their office as if it were a bunker. They want to see you. Not too much of you, but enough.

Never pretend to have all the answers

It is okay to say, 'I don't know'. People will respect you for it as long as – that is – they think you are going to go and find out... like yesterday!

Don't assume everyone has common sense

They haven't. I have worked with some bright lovely people who lack it. You can't necessarily plan for it – you would always be second guessing – but don't be surprised or disappointed when they show you they haven't got it. Being older doesn't mean you have it, either.

Just because you can doesn't mean you should

There are some things that are perfectly statutory but ill advised. Be sure your motives are honourable. For example, don't employ unqualified teachers because they are cheaper than qualified. Employ unqualified by all means, but do it for the right reasons – for example, try as you might, you can't recruit qualified or someone unqualified has impressed you and intends to train whilst in post.

Do a gaps analysis whenever you formally assess pupils

Yes it takes time and yes you have to do it quickly or else the information is quickly out-of-date, but it is invaluable to spot where weaknesses are emerging across the school as a result of testing.

Don't be afraid to show your ignorance

If you don't understand something, ask. We tell the children this but are less likely to do it ourselves. If you are confused by something or have never heard of something, someone else will be in the same position.

Your Future

'The Lord blessed the latter part of Job's life more than the former.'

Book of Job

How long should this first headship last? I have known colleagues move on after three years. I think such an approach lacks credibility. Ideas take time to embed in schools. They have to be tried out with different cohorts to see if they can be sustained rather than just work with some children, some staff and not others. If you are leading a primary school, I think a nice rule of thumb is to stay at least seven years – the time it takes for a cohort to pass through. But don't think you need ever move on. The 'Mr Chips scenario', where you stay forever in the one school, is sustainable – as long as you can reinvent yourself – finding new ideas and projects that will maintain your interest. You need to become the Madonna or the Rolling Stones of the headship world. How many times have these acts repackaged themselves in order to sustain people's interest in them? And make no mistake, people are going to have to stay interested in you and what you have to say.

I have known colleagues who seemingly stayed on too long. Or at least didn't seem to know that leaner years – poorer results or recruitment difficulties or funding problems – were on their way. I guess to parachute out of a school when the going gets tough is ultimately a very dishonourable way of acting: far better to stay and fight. Brave, though.

Things I don't do, that I wish I did, or could.

The first head teacher with whom I worked, visited each class every day. Some staff saw it as an irritation but many felt supported by his 'rounds'. I can remember saying at his retirement gathering that this would be something I would do. I never have. I think there are some obvious reasons. One is time; he was working in a different era when there were fewer demands on a head teacher's time. However, I think to some extent – if I am painfully honest – I know that if I tour classes each day I will find things that trouble me and I will need to do something about it. Does that sound defeatist? – maybe, a little? But I have enough in my in-tray to keep me busy without visiting classrooms every day. A learning walk each half-term throws up enough to be going on with.

I wish I was better at small talk. A colleague who worked for the military told me that every Friday there was a mess ball. Due to the regularity of such events, she became good at small talk – flitting from one person at a party to the next. It is a very useful skill to have at school social events.

A Final Note:
Things Get Easier but Never Easy

Don't make the mistake of thinking that because you have been doing the job you aren't going to make mistakes. Every day in this job presents an opportunity to shine but also to trip up. Live with your mistakes, learn from them. Certainly don't beat yourself up about them.

> **Winners never quit and quitters never win!**
>
> **Vince Lombardi** (Footballer)

Head Teacher's Calendar
Autumn Term

First Half-term	Completed
Staff training first day back and staff briefing	
Publish dates for the term to staff – including meeting programme	
Induction of new staff – policies distributed	
Publish term's dates for parents	
Publish year's dates for Governors	
Briefing for staff around medical needs led by school nurse – anaphylaxis, diabetes, asthma etc	
Annual Safeguarding Training for all staff Level 1	
Publish revised Staff Handbook	
Meet and Greet hour for parents to visit new teacher in classroom	
Fire Drill (block one exit)	
Start before and after school activities	
Health and Safety Inspection (incorporating Security)	
Launch new School Improvement Plan	
Review of finances with School Business Manager and Governors	
Complete pay reviews of staff by October 31st based on summer performance management outcomes	
Undertake lesson observations, planning and work scrutinies	
Undertake October Census	
Second Half-term	**Completed**
Ensure statutory policies are updated	
Write termly report for Governors	
Learning walk	
Arrange Parents' Evenings	
Review progress with School Improvement Plan	
Review of finances with School Business Manager and Governors	
Follow up on lesson observations, book and planning scrutinies	
Revise SEF in light of RAISE publication (November)	
Prepare Christmas celebrations	
Termly State of The Nation Letter to Parents	

Spring Term

First Half-term	Completed
Publish dates for term to parents	
Publish dates for staff including meeting programme	
Undertake January Census	
Fire Drill (block a different exit)	
Health and Safety Inspection (Incorporating Security)	
Make applications for variations in summer SATs	
Review of Finances with School Business Manager and Governors	
Undertake lesson observations, planning and work scrutinies	
Second Half-term	**Completed**
Prepare new budget	
Learning walk	
Review progress with School Improvement Plan	
Review of finances with School Business Manager and Governors	
Judge and record progress with school improvement plan	
Undertake parents' evenings	
Appointments for new school year – if you know of early vacancies	
Judge and record impact of previous half-term's lesson observations, planning and work scrutinies	
Termly State of The Nation Letter to Parents	

Summer Term

First Half-term	Completed
Publish dates for term to parents	
Publish dates to staff including programme of meetings	
Appointments for new school year	
Undertake lesson observations, planning and work scrutinies	
Ensure website is compliant for new school year	
Fire Drill	
Health and Safety Inspection to incorporate annual review of risk assessments	
Staff begin writing end of year reports	
Assessment week	
Second Half-term	**Completed**
Review of progress with School Improvement Plan	
Update SEF in light of summer's results	
Start to write new school improvement plan	
Read and sign pupil reports	
Judge and record impact of previous half-term's lesson observations, planning and work scrutinies	
Complete teaching staff performance reviews and set new targets that relate to the new school improvement plan	
Open Evening	
End of Year Assembly/ Celebrations	
Termly State of The Nation Letter to Parents	

References and further reading

Belbin, R Meredith (2010) Management Teams, Routledge. (See also: www.belbin.com)

Bloom, Benjamin S et al. (1956) Taxonomy of Educational Objectives: The Classification of Educational Goals. Handbook 1: Cognitive Domain, David McKay Company

Butt, Nick (1996) The Deputy Head's Survival Guide: Everything You Need to Know to be Effective and Stay Sane, First and Best in Education.

California State University (2007) Shift Happens, YouTube video.

Catchpool, Michael and Lunt Pat (2004) 36 Easy to Use Assembly Stories, Kevin Mayhew

Covey, Stephen R (2004) The Seven Habits of Highly Effective People, Simon and Schuster.

Dahl, Roald (2013) Matilda, Puffin

Education Endowment Foundation

Gardner, Howard (1993) Multiple Intelligences, Basic Books.

Goleman, Daniel (1996) Emotional Intelligence: Why it Can Matter More Than IQ, Bloomsbury Publishing PLC.

Greenleaf, Robert K (1970) The Servant as a Leader, The Greenleaf Center.

Griffith, Andy and Burns, Mark (2012) Outstanding Teaching: Engaging Learners, Crown House Publishing.

Grosz, Stephen (2014) The Examined Life, Vintage

Hart, Betty and Risley Todd R (1999) The Social World of Children Learning to Talk, Brookes Publishing Company

Hill, Alex; Mellor, Liz, Laker, Ben, Goddard, Jules (20 October 2016) 'The one type of leader that can turn around a failing school' in Harvard Business Review.

Maxwell John C (2007) 21 Irrefutable Laws of Leadership, Thomas Nelson

Hay McBer (March 2000) Raising Achievement in our Schools: Models of
Excellence for Headteachers and Deputy Headteachers in Different Settings,
Hay McBer.

McKeown, Sal (2014) 'The creative curriculum: challenging all children' in Primary
Teacher Update, Issue 38.

Nott, Gary (2017) Modern Christian Assembly Stories, Brilliant Publications.

Orwell, George (2013) Animal Farm, Maple Press.

Rainbow Good New Bible (2009), Collins.

Riener, Cedar and Willingham, Daniel (8 September 2010) 'The myth of learning
styles' in Change: The Magazine of Higher Learning (Volume 42, 2010 – Issue 5)

Ryan, Will (2008) Leadership with a Moral Purpose: Turning Your School Inside
Out, Crown House Publishing.

Acknowledgements

The author and publishers are grateful to following for allowing us to use the following:

Page 37 – 'The Leader' from Sky in the Pie by Roger McGough reprinted by permission of Peters Fraser & Dunlop (www.petersfraserdunlop.com) on behalf of Roger McGough

Page 38–39 – Free domain images used courtesy of Commons.wikipedia.org
King James I of England and VI of Scotland, by Daniel Mytens, 1621.
FDR-Library, Photos of WW2 Collection: Churchill in Quebec, 1944-23-0201a-3
Portrait of Henry VIII by the workshop of Hans Holbein the Younger, 1537.
Portrait of Charles I, Daniel Mytens the Elder, circa 1623.

Page 120 – Michael Rosen (1997), Taken from 'The Project' page 74 *The Hypnotiser*. Scholastic

Page 121 – Shenfield St Mary's Academy, Exciting Egyptians term plan

Page 160 – Havering School's Health and Safety Team, Risk Assessment Annual Review form

And a very big 'Thank you' to St Bede's Catholic Primary School and Nursery, all staff and colleagues all of whom now form part of my experiences that I'm sharing with you!

Lightning Source UK Ltd.
Milton Keynes UK
UKHW020330100521
383372UK00006BA/220

9 781783 173006